The Semisove

The Semisovereign People

A Realist's View of Democracy in America

E. E. SCHATTSCHNEIDER

Reissued with an Introduction by
David Adamany

The Dryden Press
Hinsdale, Illinois

To Ellen, Donald, and James

Grateful acknowledgement is made to the following:
P. F. Collier & Son, for permission to quote from the description by Frank
Aretas Haskell, published in Volume 43 of *The Harvard Classics* by P. F.
Collier & Son, New York, N.Y.

The New Republic for permission to quote from "Washington Wire" by
T.R.B., published in the April 6, 1959, issue of *The New Republic.*

Morton Hunt and *The New Yorker* for permission to quote from "The Ordeal of John Charles Fremont," published in the November 3, 1956, issue of
The New Yorker.

56789-065-987654321

Library of Congress Catalog Card Number: 74-25215

ISBN: 0-03-013366-1

Printed in the United States of America

Preface

THIS book started out to be an attempt to formulate a theory of political organization. While the emphasis has shifted somewhat in the course of the writing, it is still a book about political organization, an attempt to work out a theory about the relation between organization and conflict, the relation between political organization and democracy, and the organizational alternatives open to the American people. The assumption made throughout is that the nature of political organization depends on the conflicts exploited in the political system, which ultimately is what politics is about. The thesis is that we shall never understand politics unless we know what the struggle is about.

The great problem in American politics is: What makes things happen? We might understand the dynamics of American politics if we knew what is going on when things are happening. What is the process of change? What does change look like? These questions are worth asking because obviously tremendous things are going on in American public affairs, even in quiet times.

While we were thinking about something else a new government was created in the United States, so easily and quietly that most of us were wholly unaware of what was going on. Changes in the system are so great that Calvin Coolidge

would be utterly bewildered by the Washington scene today. American government has become a global operation.
We have troops stationed in Germany in peacetime. The
fleet is in the Mediterranean. United States military bases
ring the world. All has been done in spite of a strong isola-
tionist political tradition, in spite of intense opposition to the
expansion of governmental functions, in spite of strenuous
opposition to high taxes and in spite of a labyrinthine governmental structure almost perfectly designed for obstruc-
tion. As a matter of fact, the changes in the regime could
hardly have been greater if we had had a violent revolution.
How did it happen?

We are in the habit of thinking that American government is a highly stable structure supported by a public that
is strongly traditional and conservative. Evidently this is not
true. The system seems to be highly flexible.

To understand why Americans generally have been unconscious of the process of change it is necessary to take a
new look at the dynamics of American politics. Throughout
this book the emphasis has been on the dynamic character
of the American political system. The concepts formulated
here constitute an attack on all political theories, all research techniques and concepts tending to show that American politics is a meaningless stalemate about which no one
can do anything. Because so much is going on, one object of
the book is to show the need for a new public policy about
politics.

The author acknowledges with gratitude the generosity of
the Rockefeller Foundation and Wesleyan University whose
assistance made possible the writing of this volume.
                                                    —E. E. S.

Contents

Introduction

BY DAVID ADAMANY

The Political Scientist as Democrat

E. E. Schattschneider would have rejoiced in the changing mood of political studies, which has rekindled interest in *The Semisovereign People* and prompted this new edition. Political scientists who have lavished time and attention on describing political institutions and processes, on gathering and analyzing data, and on formulating testable hypotheses about political phenomena are now turning to the implications of their studies for self-government. Criticism and recommendation increasingly join description and inform it.

This is exactly the political science to which Schattschneider devoted a lifetime of teaching and writing. At the outset of his career, he was sharply critical of political science for its blind devotion to the study of legal institutions and doctrines and of classical political philosophy. In *Party Government*, he warned that lawyerly analysis had denied Americans an understanding of political parties because the

parties are mainly informal rather than legal institutions.[1]
He also complained that political philosophers, enraptured
by classical definitions of democracy embedded in Greek
city-states, had failed to formulate a statement of democracy
relevant to mass government in modern nation-states. The
organization and channeling of citizen power necessary in
modern nations is "the great omission in the theory of democracy formulated by classical philosophers who dealt exclusively with imaginary democracies," he said.[2] Later he
would renew his criticism of political philosophy for explaining the creation of democracies by such fictions as the social
contract. "Philosophers have beguiled us with tales about
the origin of government as convincing as the fables we tell
children about where babies come from," he protested.[3]

Modern students of politics, swept up in postwar scien-
tism, did not escape Schattschneider's insistence that schol-
arship aid Americans in self-government by addressing itself
to the theory and practice of democracy. The collection and
manipulation of data (in pale imitation of the natural sci-
ences) with nothing more drew Schattschneider's most bit-
ing comments. He wryly reported in his study of political
words that in 1815 empiricism was defined as "a form of
quackery."[4] And he caustically described modern political
science as "a mountain of data surrounding a vacuum."[5]
Schattschneider's belief that political scientists were inti-
mately involved and implicated in their studies was best
expressed in his reply to a student journalist who asked
whether he felt like an entomologist studying an anthill.
"No, like an ant studying an anthill," he rejoined.

No one should mistakenly believe that Schattschneider
was hostile to political analysis, however. He gathered and
applied socioeconomic data on interest group members to
demonstrate the "business and upper-class bias of the pressure system."[6] He used voting studies to demonstrate "the

law of the imperfect political mobilization of social groups,"
showing that interest groups vastly exaggerated their electoral prowess.[7] And he employed illustrative numerical examples for his now-famous analysis that the combination of
single-member districts and plurality elections bolstered the
two-party system and discriminated against "third, fourth,
and fifth parties . . . to the point of extinguishing their
chance of winning any seats altogether."[8] In each case, however, Schattschneider's empirical analysis had some broader
purpose: to show that pressure groups were not a sound
vehicle for popular democracy, that parties and officials
need not be so responsive to interest-group pressures, and
that the two-party system was stable enough to withstand
reforms that would overlay party divisions with ideological
coherence.

Schattschneider did not believe that political analysis
could be value-free, just as he did not believe it should be.
Long before modern radicals made their assault on the neutrality of contemporary political science, Schattschneider
had warned that "it is usually much more difficult to discover the right question than it is to find the answer. It is precisely at this point that the unexamined and unstated assumptions we make are most likely to defeat us, for the
questions we ask grow out of the assumptions we make. . . .
The assumptions we make tend to determine what we in-
vestigate, what kind of techniques we use, and how we evaluate the evidence."[9]

For Schattschneider, the "right question" for political scientists in a free nation was clear enough, and from it flowed
the opportunity to generate and test hypotheses about politics and then to evaluate political institutions and processes.
"The most legitimate question to be asked in a democracy
is:—how can people get control of the government? In any
other kind of system, this question cannot be asked at all."[10]

The Semisovereign People, like all of Schattschneider's writing, responds to that "most legitimate question" for political scientists in a democracy.

The Moral Premise Underlying Democracy

Insistent that the value assumptions of research be laid bare, Schattschneider nonetheless assumed the value of democracy, without laying bare his assumptions about it, until the last writing of his long career. The chronological reader of his work must wait for *Two Hundred Million Americans in Search of a Government,* published in 1969, to understand fully the commitment to democracy that informed Schattschneider's writing and research. The wait is rewarding.

In the modern, scientific era, justifications for democracy have tended toward calculations of self-interest. So it is with the argument that the participation of all in government serves the self-interest of each by warding off absolute power over his fate by others and preserving for himself some voice, albeit small, in these decisions. Similarly "practical" is the view that the participation of all contributes to a stable society, each feeling bound to governmental decisions by his own participation and each free from the uncertainties implicit in the overthrow of governments.

Schattschneider would have none of it. His faith reaffirmed a humane tradition of western political thought. The foundation for democracy is not to be found in self-interest. Simply put, *"democracy is first a state of mind."*[11] It "begins as *an act of imagination about people."*[12] This act of imagination is embodied in the Judeo-Christian tradition, the culture of ancient Greece, the common law, the history of western Europe, the Gettysburg Address, and a host of other sources that have shaped American thought. The essence of democracy as a moral system is the recognition that men are equal—*"equal in the one dimension that counts: each is a human being, infinitely precious because he is human."*[13]

Because of his profound contributions to the theory of conflict, E. E. Schattschneider has been dubbed a "conflict theorist," one of those facile categories that dominate political science. Such labeling misses Schattschneider's underlying moral premise about democracy. From the "infinitely precious" worth of every human arises the moral imperative of democratic societies. "As a moral system democracy is an experiment in the creation of a community. . . ."[14] Conflicts in democratic politics, arising as the people struggle by majority vote to get control of the government, are confined by the context of a community consensus stemming from an act of imagination of democratic citizens toward one another. "To put it very bluntly, democracy is about the *love* of people."[15]

The democracy of E. E. Schattschneider must, of course, face the paradox of majority rule and minority rights. An infinitely precious human possesses dignity and rights. At the same time, the equality of all such humans within a democratic community necessarily implies that decision-making shall be by the greater number of them. And majorities may sometimes trammel the dignity and rights of individuals. Nonetheless, Schattschneider explicitly favored majority rule and regarded such institutionalized minority vetoes as the separation of powers as barriers to popular government.[16] "There is no democratic reason for slighting the *rule* in majority rule," he said.[17]

Civil liberties do not contradict majority-rule democracy in Schattschneider's world. Indeed, freedom of speech, press, and association are essential to the creation of community: the process of education that must continually occur in successful democracies to permit minorities to seek majority status and to allow majorities to persuade minorities to consent to their decisions.[18] At the same time, minority rights are safeguarded by the beliefs essential for a democratic community. The infinitely precious worth of equal citizens and the love of fellow men compel majorities to respect individual liberty.

Democracy is based on a profound insight into human nature, the realization that all men are sinful, all are imperfect, all are prejudiced, and none knows the whole truth. That is why we need liberty and why we have an obligation to hear all men. Liberty gives us a chance to learn from other people, to become aware of our own limitations, and to correct our bias. Even when we disagree with other people we like to think that they speak from good motives, and while we realize that all men are limited, we do not let ourselves image that any man is bad. Democracy is a political system for people who are not sure that they are right.[19]

Love for others makes freedom possible, and recognition of one's own limitations makes it necessary.

The Citizen and Democracy

Although he exalted the worth of each individual, Schattschneider took a modest view of the democratic citizen. He objected to portraying democratic citizens as supermen. The problem of defining citizens' obligations arose because "the controversy about democracy . . . antedates the rise of modern democracy" and "the main lines of the argument were laid down long before anyone had ever seen a real modern democratic government at work."[20] Consequently, as the nation-state emerged, democrats continued to think in classical terms. Democracy was defined as "government by the people."

But the classical model of the small city-state has little

relevance to modern nations. In Greek democracies, there were few citizens; supported by a large slave class, they had leisure time for politics; the issues were relatively simple; the organization of government was straightforward; and direct participation by all was possible. In modern nations, however, there are millions of citizens; their days are occupied earning a living and meeting private obligations; public issues are complex and numerous; government structures are sprawling and mazelike; and community meetings of the whole citizenry are impossible.

The classical concept of government, of popular sovereignty exercised by direct participation in affairs, was kept alive during the rise of American democracy by the influential writings of Jean Jacques Rousseau, by the example of New England town meetings, and by the rhetoric of revered politicans like Lincoln, who continually reviewed the image of "government by the people."[21] Political thinkers failed to reassess the proper role of citizens in modern democracy, with disastrous effects for political theory. "So certain were the philosophers that the people would in fact use their new powers of self-government that the whole controversy over democracy has concentrated on the competence of the masses to direct public affairs. At this point oceans of ink have been wasted. . . ."[22]

The advent of opinion polls seemed to turn the issue against democracy. Researchers soon discovered that more citizens could identify sports figures and movie stars than could name Cabinet officers and leading politicians, that only 43 percent could name their congressman, that only 19 percent knew how he had voted on any bill, and so forth. The masses were judged incompetent to direct public affairs.

Schattschneider warned that such research went awry precisely because of its unstated assumptions. In *The Semi-*

sovereign People he denounced "the implication that democracy is a failure because the people are too ignorant to
answer intelligently all the questions asked by pollsters. This
is a professorial invention for imposing professorial standards on the political system. . . . Who, after all, are these
self-appointed censors who assume that they are in a position to flunk the whole human race? . . . Democracy was
made for the people, not the people for democracy. Democracy is something for ordinary people, . . . regardless of
whether or not the pedants approve of them."[23]

It was not democratic citizens who failed, Schattschneider
insisted, but political scientists and philosophers. "The crisis
here is not a crisis in democracy but a crisis in theory."[24] It is
foolish to argue that democracy must educate and interest
everyone in politics so that voters can think about politics
the way a United States senator might think about it.[25]

The whole theory of knowledge implicit in such demands
on citizens falsifies the reality of modern life. People survive
in the contemporary world by distinguishing between what
they must know and what they do not need to know or
cannot know. In their private lives they are required to
"place confidence daily in a thousand ways in pharmacists,
surgeons, pilots, bank clerks, engineers, plumbers, technicians, lawyers. . . . They realize that it is not necessary to
know how to *make* a television set in order to buy one intelligently."[26]

Similarly, the people cannot know enough actually to govern. Indeed, "there is no escape from the problem of ignorance, because *nobody knows enough to run the government.*"[27] Public officials know only slightly more than the
ordinary citizen, and one who becomes an expert fails the
classical test of citizenship because "an expert is a person
who chooses to be ignorant about many things so that he
may know all about one."[28] The role of the citizen in public

affairs is, therefore, the same as in private matters. In both,
"our survival depends on our ability to judge things by their
results and our ability to establish relations of confidence
and responsibility so that we can take advantage of what
other people know."[29]

Hence there is a need to redefine democracy, making it
consistent with what the people are able and willing to do
and to know in the complex modern world. Jefferson's model of "government by consent of the governed" is much
more realistic in such a world than is the classical definition
of "government by the people."[30] Democracy, then, "is like
nearly everything else we do; it is a form of collaboration of
ignorant people and experts."[31] This collaboration necessarily involves leaders as well as followers, representation rather than direct democracy, and choice rather than participation. In the nation-state, therefore:

> *Democracy is a competitive political system in which competing*
> *leaders and organizations define the alternatives of public policy*
> *in such a way that the public can participate in the decision-mak-*
> *ing process. . . .*
>
> Conflict, competition, organization, leadership, and responsibili-
> ty are the ingredients of a working definition of democracy.[32]

Consistent with this "working definition" of modern democracy, Schattschneider devoted himself to writing about the
institutions of organization and leadership—namely political
parties and interest groups—and about the process of conflict and change.

Political Parties, Pressure Groups, and Democracy

Assessing his own work, Schattschneider once said, "I suppose the most important thing I have done in my field is

that I have talked longer and harder and more persistently and enthusiastically about political parties than anyone else alive."[33] Although too modest an evaluation, these comments reflect Schattschneider's belief that political parties are the essential institution of organization and leadership that make democracy possible. Political parties, he said, "characteristically undertake to get control of the government by nominating candidates and electing them to office; the object is to get power by winning elections."[34] This is a majoritarian process, and a party mandated by majority vote can lay claim to both the authority and the legitimacy to rule.

Pressure groups, by sharp contrast, "seek to accomplish specific, relatively narrow tasks, to influence policy at selected points, and do not aim at winning the general power to govern."[35] They are not majoritarian, and they may not claim legitimate power to govern in a democracy. "The distinguishing mark of pressure tactics is not merely that it does not seek to win elections, but that in addition it does not attempt to persuade a majority. . . . Pressure politics is a method of short-circuiting the majority."[36] These observations put Schattschneider at loggerheads with a generation of American political scientists, who praised group politics as the manifestation of America's multitude of interests and who believed that pluralism—the governance by groups in coalition—both represented the people and prevented the tyranny of the majority.

Schattschneider's disdain for the "groupists" is especially clear in *The Semisovereign People*. He warned of the probusiness and upper-class bias of the pressure group system.[37] He artfully employed the data of political science to show that business and the upper-classes are more likely to organize for politics; that they have greater political resources, such as money and prestige; and that their small numbers tend to dominate interest-group politics. "The flaw in the pluralist heaven is that the heavenly chorus sings with a strong upper-class accent. Probably about 90 percent of the people cannot get into the pressure system."[38]

The tactics of special interest groups also distort democracy and thwart majority rule, as Schattschneider painstakingly pointed out in his celebrated study of the tariff.[39] The method of giving notice and conducting congressional hearings favors established lobbyists. Privileged groups often obtained semiconfidential information from congressmen about the development of legislation.[40] Pressure groups exaggerate the size and unanimity of their membership, usually without congressional challenge.[41] And group spokesmen often represented positions to Congress that had not been endorsed by the whole membership.[42]

Most important, however, is the assumption of interest-group theorists that politics consists of conflict between the special interests. "The diet on which the American leviathan feeds is something more than a jungle of disparate special interests,"[43] Schattschneider warned. There is also a public interest. It encompasses, first, "the common interest in seeing that there is fair play among private interests"[44] and "the body of common agreement . . . known as the 'consensus,' without which . . . no democratic system can survive."[45]

Beyond these agreed rules of the democratic game, however, is a broad public interest in certain issues upon which turn the nation's very survival. "The nature of modern public policy (economic stabilization, control of inflation, war mobilization of the economy, the integration of defense and foreign policy), creates a new kind of politics. . . . The distinguishing characteristic of modern politics is that it is based on conflicts about the public interest rather than conflicts among special interests. It is the principal function of politics to defend the public interest."[46] This public interest is not fixed or certain, because citizens will disagree on the nation's best approach to them.[47] But the public interest does entail citizens' thinking about the best policy *for the nation* rather than the narrow striving for self-interest that characterizes interest-group theory and activity.

The alternative to special-interest politics is party politics. "Party government is good democratic doctrine because the parties are the special form of political organization adapted to the mobilization of majorities."[48] Parties should lay down programs, submit them to the people, and then carry out those programs if given an electoral mandate. In mass democracy, "the people are a sovereign whose vocabulary is limited to two words, 'yes' and 'no'. This sovereign, moreover, can speak only when spoken to."[49] It is up to the parties to state the propositions to which the voters may respond with approval or disapproval. Furthermore, this role for voters is consistent with the model of democracy based "on the consent of the governed" and does not require "government by the people," which is impossible in mass democracy.

These propositions led Schattschneider to his well-known advocacy of party reform. American political parties, he observed, "*function effectively in electing candidates to office but govern badly because they do not mobilize effectively the men they elect to office.*"[50] When parties do not mobilize to formulate and enact programs, but only to elect officials, the people are not sovereign, but only semisovereign. They do not control the government.

The failure of American parties, Schattschneider believed, was caused by sectionalism and localism, which focus attention on special interests rather than national issues; by patronage, which causes party leaders to pursue self-gain instead of a program mandated by the people; by the separation of powers—the "antiparty part of the constitutional scheme"[51]—which frustrates party attempts to grasp government and decisively direct it; by the seniority system in Congress;[52] by convention nominations, which mainly are controlled by local bosses;[53] and by primaries, which when not dominated by political machines thwart the power of voters by denying them the organization and leadership, through party labels and platforms, that allow them to effectively answer "yes" or "no" at the polls.[54]

In his own writings and in the Report of the Committee on Political Parties of the American Political Science Association,[55] which committee he chaired, Schattschneider endorsed many changes in the structure and arrangements of American politics to overcome these barriers to party government. Those proposals, often provocative, have not been adopted. More important than the specific proposals for party reform, however, was Schattschneider's belief that the changing conditions of American politics were propitious for party government. The decline of sectionalism,[56] the demise of the old-style machine,[57] the rise of class politics to replace sectional alignments,[58] the development of national interest groups—especially organized labor—which attach themselves more or less permanently to one of the party coalitions;[59] and the emergence of such issues as employment policy and foreign affairs that have nationwide impact[60]—these are the raw materials from which an issue-oriented, national, responsible two-party system might be built.

Finally, Schattschneider believed that "the greatest difficulties in the way of the development of party government in the United States have been intellectual, not legal" and "once a respectable section of the public understands the issue, ways of promoting party government through the Constitution can be found."[61] This aspiration that the people give their confidence to the parties has, like the reformers' specific proposals for change, been defeated in recent decades. Nonetheless, the changing conditions of American politics foreseen by Schattschneider have made parties more issue-oriented and more ideologically coherent, and voters have learned that the two major parties stand on different sides of the great ideological divide.[62] Though still lacking organization that can mobilize the party in government for specific policies, the American parties have probably advanced in the direction urged by Schattschneider because each is more ideologically coherent and the two are more clearly separated on major issues.

The Democratic Dynamic of Conflict

Schattschneider's objection to pressure-group government went beyond its probusiness, upper-class, and minority bias to its underlying assumption that politics is essentially static. He denounced the myth that "the pressure system is automatically representative of the whole community,"[63] and he rejected the description of politics as a " 'balance of power' among the contending groups."[64] Group theory too often "assumes that the equation of forces is fixed at the outset," and this ignores the dynamics of conflict.[65]

"The dynamics of politics has its origin in strife,"[66] Schattschneider argued; and both the process and the outcome of politics depend on four dimensions that shape conflict. First is the scope of conflict: who and how many become involved in conflict? Adding new participants to a fight changes the balance of forces and alters the outcome.[67] The scope of conflict is marked by opposing tendencies toward the "privatization" and "socialization" of conflict.[68] Private conflict is settled without the intervention of public authority: it may be resolved in terms of economic competition, private sanctions, negotiations, and so forth. "Since the contestants in private conflicts are apt to be unequal in strength, it follows that *the most powerful special interests want private settlement* because they are able to dictate the outcome as long as the conflict remains private. . . . It is the weak who want to socialize conflict, i.e., to involve more and more people in the conflict until the balance of forces is changed."[69]

Because participation in government is reasonably easy in a free society, in democracies this "flight to government [by the weak] is perpetual."[70]

Many American values support the privatization of conflict, for example, free enterprise, individualism, and privacy. Other, competing ideals support the socialization of conflict: "ideas concerning equality, consistency, equal protection of the laws, justice, liberty, freedom of movement, freedom of speech and association, and civil right. . . ."[71] Democracy is the greatest force for the socialization of conflict, because it allows the whole public to get into every conflict it wants to enter.

Visibility is a second dimension of conflict.[72] Conflict occurs more readily about issues that are visible. Historically government maintained a low profile, by emphasizing regulatory activities and "painless" taxes. But governmental responsibility for the economy and for war and peace, as well as changing governmental procedures and new modes of political combat, raise the visibility of public actions and invite greater conflict about them.

Intensity also shapes conflict.[73] American politics has historically assumed widespread public indifference. But people feel more intensely about great issues of war, foreign policy, human rights, and economic policy; and such conflicts are fought with greater intensity.

Finally, there is the direction of conflict. Many conflicts

arise, each dividing people into different factions, parties, classes, and so forth.[74] But Schattschneider is skeptical about any "equality of conflicts" which "tend to weaken all antagonisms in the community, producing a system of low-grade tensions."[75] Some conflicts displace others, because they are more visible and intense. As among conflicts, people must set priorities and fight those which are most important. Once lines of division are drawn around high-priority conflicts, each side tends to become unified. Lower-priority conflicts are submerged to maintain allegiances on high-priority issues. Those on each side of a major conflict tend to consolidate, even though they differ on lesser issues.[76] This leads to stability in politics, focused on more or less permanent majority and minority coalitions.

The dimensions of conflict are, of course, related. The most highly visible and intense conflicts tend to shape the direction, as people take up sides on the issues they know and care most about. Visibility and intensity also determine the scope of politics, because people will participate when they know and care about issues. But direction also bears on scope, for people may not become involved if the main cleavages in politics are not very relevant to them.

The dimensions of conflict set the strategy of politics. Once a direction has been set, the leaders of the majority seek continuously to exploit the cleavage in order to hold their coalition together. If the opposition merely accepts the direction of conflict, the system becomes relatively stable. But the strategy of opposition is to seek "a substitution of conflicts" by advancing other issues which exploit the submerged conflicts in the majority coalition, raising their intensity and visibility, and ultimately splitting the dominant alliance. A substitution of conflicts also alters the scope of conflict; different people are attracted to the fray by the new direction of conflict, while some who formerly participated do not care enough about the new issues to continue their efforts.

The substitution or displacement of conflicts, then, is the heart of political strategy. Republicans recently have been urged to exploit the issues of race, welfare, crime, protest, youth life styles, and others to divide the Democratic coalition, dominant since the New Deal, which organizes national politics around economic issues.[77] Indeed, Richard Nixon successfully pursued such a strategy in 1972, winning votes of "working-class" Democrats by associating the McGovern-Shriver ticket with amnesty, abortion, and acid rather than the social-welfare and economic programs that Democrats had traditionally taken to the country. A Democratic counterstrategy plays down the social issue and permits economic issues to remain the major cleavage in electoral politics.[78]

Political leaders and parties have the responsibility for organizing conflict, by raising the visibility and intensity of conflict and by advancing the issues that set its direction. Interest groups will not do so, because the most powerful of them prefer the privatization of conflict. The traditional nonideological parties have also failed, because they have not raised the great "public-interest" issues that involve most Americans. As a result, large numbers of Americans have ignored elections, as the presence of 63 million nonvoters in 1972 attests. "The problem of nonvoting is to be found in the way in which the alternatives in American politics are defined, the way in which issues get referred to the public, the scale of competition and organization, and above all *what* issues are developed.[79]

In America the nonvoters are drawn disproportionately from among the young, the poor, and the racial minorities for whom the direction of politics set by traditional interest groups and nonprogrammatic parties holds little interest. In 1960, Schattschneider warned that "the present boycott . . .

has brought the political system *very near to something like the limit of tolerance of passive abstention.*"[80] Within the decade some, who reflected the frustration of the nonvoters, abandoned passive abstention and took their case into the streets. *"The definition of the alternatives is the supreme instrument of power,"*[81] and the failure of parties and leadership to define alternatives suitable to a vast segment of the nation had left them powerless and ultimately led them to reject democratic means.

Later, in *Two Hundred Million Americans in Search of a Government*, Schattschneider would somewhat modify his emphasis on decisive action by majoritarian political institutions. "The life of the nation is the source of politics. . . . The cycle is apt to begin in the private sector because that is where almost anyone can make a beginning by himself. The private life of the community is the breeding ground of millions of initiatives; later when the chain reaction gets out of hand the government is involved."[82]

"Why Is a Generation the Proper Period of Time for the Study of Politics?" Schattschneider asked.[83] Because "ideas govern the world."[84] Delay is inherent in such a process, for the socialization of private agitation takes a long time. Ideas must be expounded and introduced into the public arena; they must be shaped and reshaped in search of a majority; and in a noncoercive democracy, the minority must continue to be persuaded of ideas even after they have lost the vote.[85] "Much of the sense of frustration that people feel about the American political system is due to the fact that they take a very short-range view of the political process."[86]

Nonetheless, leadership and parties remain important. They set the direction of conflict and thereby determine its scope by the alternatives they select from the millions of private initiatives to present to the people. American democracy has still not faced Schattschneider's essential question: "How can people get control of the government?" Neither leadership nor organization has set the visibility, intensity, and direction of politics so as to broaden its scope to the whole people. Coherent alternatives are still not referred to the people in ways that allow them to endorse or reject programs and leaders within the limits inherent in a mass democracy. There remains still a vacuum in translating popular mandates into governmental action. Conflict is central to self-government, and Schattschneider's warning that we have not organized conflict to allow the people to get control of the government rings as plainly today as it did during his lifetime.

In Retrospect

E. E. Schattschneider (1892-1971) was first a democratic philosopher and partisan, and he was a political scientist only as far as being so was useful in discovering and advocating means by which the people could get control of the government. His writing was all directed to that overriding purpose. So was his teaching. Although he was a distinguished political scientist, who served as President of the American Political Science Association (1956-57), he chose, after a brief start elsewhere, to teach Wesleyan University undergraduates for the duration of his long career. He preferred talking to young people about the democracy they would make for themselves to following the narrower path of academic professionalism by teaching graduate students. Schattschneider urged young people to become involved in politics, and he was a central figure in the National Center for Education in Politics, which sponsored governmental internships for students.

Schattschneider followed his own advice, serving on the

Middletown City Council, the State Election Laws Commission, the State Board of Mediation and Arbitration, and the State Board of Pardons. Both his political activity and his intellectual life, each marked by strong views, nonetheless reflected the humane temperament that was the foundation of his democratic philosophy. His Wesleyan colleagues would describe him posthumously as a "seminal writer on American politics, compelling teacher, irrepressible raconteur, guiding force in professional associations, and political activist."[87]

Schattschneider's legacy is greater than his well-known contributions about pressure groups, political parties, and conflict. It lies in his insistence that we continually ask ourselves how, in modern democracy, the people can get control of the government. And it lies in the moral bias that underlay his confidence in democracy. He stood squarely in the western philosophic and religious tradition that treasured the inherent worth of each man; and he combined this moral assumption with an Enlightenment belief in the capacity of men to make intelligent collective decisions by a process of rational discourse. All of Schattschneider's political science was built on these ethical assumptions. This temper of his work was best captured in his epitaph for another.

He paid us the great compliment of thinking that we were interested in public affairs and could understand what politics was about. . . . He did not think the way to a man's heart was through his stomach; he thought the way to a man's heart was through his head. To him, democracy made sense because public discussion might be used to enlighten the people.

University of Wisconsin

Notes

1. *Party Government* (New York: Holt, Rinehart and Winston, 1942), pp. 11-16.
2. *Party Government*, p. 14.
3. *Two Hundred Million Americans in Search of a Government* (New York: Holt, Rinehart and Winston, 1969), p.5.
4. *Two Hundred Million Americans*, p. 103.
5. *Two Hundred Million Americans*, p. 8.
6. *The Semisovereign People* (first published Holt, Rinehart and Winston, 1960), pp. 30-36.
7. *Semisovereign People*, pp. 49-52. Also, *Party Government*, pp. 33-34.
8. *Party Government*, pp. 67-90, quote at p.75.
9. *The Struggle for Party Government* (College Park: University of Maryland, 1948), p. 21. All quoted italics from original text.
10. *Struggle for Party Government*, pp. 22.
11. *Two Hundred Million Americans*, p. 42.
12. *Two Hundred Million Americans*, p. 46.
13. *Two Hundred Million Americans*, p. 45.
14. *Two Hundred Million Americans*, p. 47.
15. *Two Hundred Million Americans*, p. 43.
16. *Party Government*, p. 7.
17. *Struggle for Party Government*, p. 9.
18. *Two Hundred Million Americans*, p. 88.
19. *Two Hundred Million Americans*, p. 54.
20. *Party Government*, p. 13.
21. *Two Hundred Million Americans*, pp. 58-61.
22. *Party Government*, pp. 14-15.
23. *Semisovereign People*, p. 135.
24. *Semisovereign People*, p. 134.
25. *Semisovereign People*, p. 133.
26. *Semisovereign People*, p. 137.
27. *Semisovereign People*, p. 136.
28. *Semisovereign People*, pp. 136-137.
29. *Semisovereign People*, p. 137.
30. *Two Hundred Million Americans*, p. 58.
31. *Semisovereign People*, p. 137.
32. *Semisovereign People*, p. 141.
33. *Wesleyan Argus*, March 5, 1971, p. 2.
34. "Pressure Groups versus Political Parties," *The Annals*, 259 (September, 1948), 17.
35. *Party Government*, pp. 187-188.
36. *Party Government*, p. 189.
37. *Semisovereign People*, pp. 30-36.
38. *Semisovereign People*, p. 35.
39. *Politics, Pressures and the Tariff* (New York: Prentice-Hall, 1935).
40. *Politics, Pressures and the Tariff*, pp. 164-184.
41. *Politics, Pressures and the Tariff*, pp. 226-249.

42. *Politics, Pressures and the Tariff*, pp. 271-278.

43. *Semisovereign People*, p. 23.

44. "Political Parties and the Public Interest," *The Annals*, 280 (March, 1952), 22.

45. *Semisovereign People*, p. 23.

46. "Political Parties and the Public Interest," p. 23.

47. "Political Parties and the Public Interest," p. 23.

48. *Party Government*, p. 208.

49. *Party Government*, p. 52.

50. *Party Government*, p. 29.

51. *Party Government*, p. 7.

52. For these analyses of antiparty elements, see *Party Government*, pp. 7-9, 111-123, 133-140, and 141-142.

53. For this discussion of convention nominations, see *Party Government*, pp. 99-106.

54. *Party Government*, pp. 53-61.

55. Committee on Political Parties, "Toward a More Responsible Two-Party System," *American Political Science Review*, 44 (September, 1950), Supplement.

56. "1954: The Ike Party Fights to Live," *New Republic*, February 23, 1953, pp. 15-17. Also, "United States: The Functional Approach to Party Government," *Modern Political Parties*, ed. Sigmund Neuman (Chicago: University of Chicago Press, 1956), pp. 209-214.

57. "Functional Approach to Party Government," p. 214.

58. "1954: The Ike Party Fights to Live," pp. 16-17.

59. "Functional Approach to Party Government," pp. 213-214.

60. "Party Government and Employment Policy," *American Political Science Review*, 39 (December, 1945), 1147-1157; "Functional Approach to Party Government," pp. 208, 213; *Semisovereign People*, pp. 88-89.

61. *Party Government*, pp. 209-210.

62. See, for instance, Gerald M. Pomper, "From Confusion to Clarity: Issues and American Voters, 1956-1968," *American Political Science Review*, 66 (June, 1972), 415-428.

63. *Semisovereign People*, p. 35.

64. *Semisovereign People*, p. 37.

65. *Semisovereign People*, p. 39.

66. "Intensity, Visibility, Direction and Scope," *American Political Science Review* 51 (December, 1957), 935.

67. "Intensity, Visibility, Direction and Scope," pp. 941-942; *Semisovereign People*, pp. 2-3.

68. *Semisovereign People*, p. 7.

69. *Semisovereign People*, p. 40.

70. *Semisovereign People*, p. 40.

71. *Semisovereign People*, p. 7.

72. "Intensity, Visibility, Direction and Scope," p. 938.

73. "Intensity, Visibility, Direction and Scope," p. 938.

74. "Intensity, Visibility, Direction and Scope," pp. 939-941.

75. *Semisovereign People*, p. 67.

76. *Semisovereign People*, p. 64.

77. Kevin P. Phillips, *The Emerging Republican Majority* (New Rochelle, New York: Arlington House, 1969).

78. Richard Scammon and Ben J. Wattenberg, *The Real Majority* (New York: Coward-McCann, 1970).

79. *Semisovereign People*, p. 110.

80. *Semisovereign People*, p. 109.

81. *Semisovereign People*, p. 68.

82. *Two Hundred Million Americans*, p. 93.

83. *Two Hundred Million Americans*, Chapter 5.

84. *Two Hundred Million Americans*, p. 991.

85. *Two Hundred Million Americans*, Chapter 5.

86. *Two Hundred Million Americans*, p. 81.

87. Fred I. Greenstein and Clement E. Vose, "Elmer Eric Schattschneider," *PS* 4 (Summer, 1971), 503.

1

The Contagiousness
of Conflict

On a hot afternoon in August, 1943, in the Harlem section of New York City, a Negro soldier and a white policeman got into a fight in the lobby of a hotel. News of the fight spread rapidly throughout the area. In a few minutes angry crowds gathered in front of the hotel, at the police station, and at the hospital to which the injured policeman was taken. Before order could be restored, about four hundred people were injured and millions of dollars' worth of property was destroyed.

This was not a race riot. Most of the shops looted and the property destroyed by the Negro mob belonged to Negroes. As a matter of fact neither the white policeman nor the Negro soldier had anything to do with the riot they had set off; they did not participate in it, did not control it, and knew nothing about it.

Fortunately for the survival of American civilization conflict rarely erupts as violently as it did in the 1943 Harlem riot, but all conflict has about it some elements that go into the making of a riot. Nothing attracts a crowd so quickly as a fight. Nothing is so contagious. Parliamentary debates, jury trials, town meetings, political campaigns, strikes, hearings, all have about them some of the exciting qualities of a fight; all produce dramatic spectacles that are almost irresistibly

1

fascinating to people. At the root of all politics is the universal language of conflict.

The central political fact in a free society is the tremendous contagiousness of conflict.

Every fight consists of two parts: (1) the few individuals
who are actively engaged at the center and (2) the audience
that is irresistibly attracted to the scene. The spectators are
as much a part of the over-all situation as are the overt combatants. The spectators are an integral part of the situation,
for, as likely as not, the *audience* determines the outcome of
the fight. The crowd is loaded with portentousness because
it is apt to be a hundred times as large as the fighting minority, and the relations of the audience and the combatants
are highly unstable. Like all other chain reactions, a fight is
difficult to contain. To understand any conflict it is necessary therefore to keep constantly in mind the relations between the combatants and the audience because the audience is likely to do the kinds of things that determine the
outcome of the fight. This is true because the audience is
overwhelming; it is never really neutral; the excitement of
the conflict communicates itself to the crowd. *This is the
basic pattern of all politics.*

The first proposition is that the outcome of every conflict
is determined by the *extent* to which the audience becomes
involved in it. That is, the outcome of all conflict is determined by the *scope* of its contagion. The number of people
involved in any conflict determines what happens; every
change in the number of participants, every increase or reduction in the number of participants, affects the result.
Simply stated, the first proposition is that the intervention
of Cole into a conflict between Able and Bart inevitably
changes the nature of the conflict. Cole may join Able and
tip the balance of forces in his favor, or he may support Bart
and turn the balance the other way, or he may disrupt the

conflict or attempt to impose his own resolution on both Able and Bart. No matter what he does, however, Cole will alter the conflict by transforming a one-to-one contest into a two-to-one conflict or a triangular conflict. Thereafter every new intervention, by Donald, Ellen, Frank, James, Emily, will alter the equation merely by enlarging the scope of conflict because each addition changes the balance of the forces involved. Conversely, every abandonment of the conflict by any of the participants changes the ratio.

The moral of this is: If a fight starts, watch the crowd, because the crowd plays the decisive role.

At the nub of politics are, first, the way in which the public participates in the spread of the conflict and, second, the processes by which the unstable relation of the public to the conflict is controlled.

The second proposition is a consequence of the first. The most important strategy of politics is concerned with the scope of conflict.

So great is the change in the nature of any conflict likely to be as a consequence of the widening involvement of people in it that the original participants are apt to lose control of the conflict altogether. Thus, Able and Bart may find, as the Harlem policeman and soldier found, that the fight they started has got out of hand and has been taken over by the audience. Therefore the contagiousness of conflict, the elasticity of its scope and the fluidity of the involvement of people are the X factors in politics.

Implicit in the foregoing propositions is another: It is extremely unlikely that both sides will be reinforced equally as the scope of the conflict is doubled or quadrupled or multiplied by a hundred or a thousand. That is, the balance of the forces recruited will almost certainly not remain constant. This is true because it is improbable that the participants in the original conflict constitute a representative sample of the larger community; nor is it likely that the successive increments are representative. Imagine what might happen if there were a hundred times as many spectators on the fringes of the conflict who sympathized with Able rather than Bart. Able would have a strong motive for trying to spread the conflict while Bart would have an overwhelming interest in keeping it private. It follows that conflicts are frequently won or lost by the success that the contestants have in getting the audience involved in the fight or in excluding it, as the case may be.

Other propositions follow. It is one of the qualities of extremely small conflicts that the relative strengths of the contestants are likely to be known in advance. In this case the stronger side may impose its will on the weaker without an overt test of strength because people are apt not to fight if they are sure to lose. This is extremely important because the scope of conflict can be most easily restricted at the very beginning. On the other hand, the weaker side may have a great potential strength provided only that it can be aroused. The stronger contestant may hesitate to use his strength because he does not know whether or not he is going to be able to isolate his antagonist. Thus, the bystanders are a part of the calculus of all conflicts. And any attempt to forecast the outcome of a fight by estimating the strength of the original contestants is likely to be fatuous.

Every change in the scope of conflict has a bias; it is partisan in its nature. That is, it must be assumed that every change in the number of participants is about something, that the newcomers have sympathies or antipathies that make it possible to involve them. By definition, the intervening bystanders are not neutral. Thus, in political conflict every change in scope changes the equation.

The logical consequence of the foregoing analysis of conflict is that the balance of forces in any conflict is not a fixed equation until *everyone* is involved. If one tenth of 1 percent of the public is involved in conflict, the latent force of the audience is 999 times as great as the active force, and the outcome of the conflict depends overwhelmingly on what the 99.9 percent do. Characteristically, the potentially involved are more numerous than those actually involved. This analysis has a bearing on the relations between the "interested" and the "uninterested" segments of the community and sheds light on interest theories of politics. It is hazardous to assume that the spectators are uninterested because a free society maximizes the contagion of conflict; it invites intervention and gives a high priority to the participation of the public in conflict.

The foregoing statement is wholly theoretical and analytical. Is there any connection between the theory outlined here and what actually happens in politics? Since theoretically control of the scope of conflict is absolutely crucial, is there any evidence that politicians, publicists, and men of affairs are actually aware of this factor? Do politicians in the real world try to reallocate power by managing the scope of conflict? These questions are important because they may shed light on the dynamics of politics, on what actually happens in the political process, and on what can or cannot be accomplished in the political system. In other words, the role of the scope of conflict in politics is so great that it makes necessary a new interpretation of the political system.

If it is true that the result of political contests is determined by the scope of public involvement in conflicts, much that has been written about politics becomes nonsense, and we are in for a revolution in our thinking about politics. The scope factor overthrows the familiar simplistic calculus based on the model of a tug of war of measurable forces. One is reminded of the ancient observation that the battle is not necessarily won by the strong nor the race by the swift. The scope factor opens up vistas of a new kind of political universe.

In view of the highly strategic character of politics we ought not to be surprised that the instruments of strategy are likely to be important in inverse proportion to the amount of public attention given to them.[1]

Madison understood something about the relation of scope to the outcome of conflict. His famous essay No. 10 in the *Federalist Papers* should be reread in the context of this discussion.

The smaller the society, the fewer probably will be the distinct parties and interests composing it, the more frequently will a majority be found of the same party; and the smaller number of individuals composing a majority, and the smaller the compass within which they are placed, the more easily they will concert and execute their plans of oppression. Extend the sphere and you take in a greater variety of parties and interests; you make it less probable that a majority of the whole will have a common motive to invade the rights of other citizens.

While Madison saw some of the elements of the situation, no one has followed up his lead to develop a general theory. The question of the scope of conflict is approached obliquely in the literature of political warfare. The debate is apt to deal with *procedural questions* which have an unavowed bearing on the question. The very fact that the subject is handled so gingerly is evidence of its explosive potential.

While there is no explicit formulation in the literature of American politics of the principle that the scope of a conflict determines its outcome, there is a vast amount of controversy that can be understood only in the light of this proposition. That is, throughout American history tremendous efforts have been made to control the scope of conflict, but the rationalizations of the efforts are interesting chiefly because they have been remarkably confusing. Is it possible to reinterpret American politics by exposing the unavowed factor in these discussions?

A look at political literature shows that there has indeed been *a long-standing struggle between the conflicting tendencies toward the privatization and socialization of conflict.* On the one hand, it is easy to identify a whole battery of ideas calculated to restrict the scope of conflict or even to keep it entirely out of the public domain. A long list of ideas concerning individualism, free private enterprise, localism, privacy, and economy in government seems to be designed to privatize conflict or to restrict its scope or to limit the use of public authority to enlarge the scope of conflict. A tremendous amount of conflict is controlled by keeping it so private that it is almost completely invisible. Reference to this strategy abounds in the literature of politics, but the rationalizations of the strategy make no allusion to the relation of these ideas to the scope of conflict. The justifications are nearly always on other grounds.

On the other hand, it is equally easy to identify another battery of ideas contributing to the socialization of conflict. Universal ideas in the culture, ideas concerning equality, consistency, equal protection of the laws, justice, liberty, freedom of movement, freedom of speech and association, and civil rights tend to socialize conflict. These concepts tend to make conflict contagious; they invite outside intervention in conflict and form the basis of appeals to public authority for redress of private grievances. Here again the rationalizations are made on grounds which do not avow any specific interest in an expansion of the scope of conflict though the relation becomes evident as soon as we begin to think about it. Scope is the unlisted guest of honor at all of these occasions.

It may be said, therefore, that men of affairs do in fact make an effort to control the scope of conflict though they usually explain what they do on some other grounds. The way the question is handled suggests that the real issue may be too hot to handle otherwise. We are bound to suppose therefore that control of the scale of conflict has always been a prime instrument of political strategy, whatever the language of politics may have been.

A better understanding of circuitous references to the strategic role of the scope factor may be gained if we examine some of the procedural issues which have been most widely debated in American politics. Do these issues have a bearing on the practical meaning of the scope conflict?

The role of conflict in the political system depends, first, on the morale, self-confidence, and security of the individuals and groups who must challenge the dominant groups in the community in order to raise an opposition.

People are not likely to start a fight if they are certain that they are going to be severely penalized for their efforts. In this situation, repression may assume the guise of a false unanimity. A classic historical instance is the isolation of the Negro in some southern communities. Dollard says of the southern caste system that "it is a way of limiting conflict between the races. . . . Middle class Negroes are especially sensitive to their isolation and feel the lack of a forum in Southern towns where problems of the two races could be discussed."[2] The controversy about civil rights in connection with race relations refers not merely to the rights of southern Negroes to protest but also to the rights of "outsiders" to intervene.

The civil rights of severely repressed minorities and all measures for public or private intervention in disputes about the status of these minorities become meaningful when we relate them to the attempt to make conflict visible. Scope is the stake in these discussions.

Attempts to impose unanimity are made in one-party areas in the North as well as in the South. Vidich and Bensman describe the process by which the school board in a small town in upstate New York undertakes to control a political situation by limiting conflict. Commenting on the procedures of the board, the authors say that it attempts to deal with critics by making "greater efforts at concealment." These efforts "result in more strict adherence to the principle of unanimity of decision."[3]

In a similar situation, in a Michigan village, "the practice of holding secret meetings was defended Monday night by Chester McGonigal, president of the Board of Education at James Couzen's Agricultural School. Mr. McGonigal said that the Bath school board would continue to hold discussion meetings closed to the public and that only decisions reached would be announced."[4]

Perhaps the whole political strategy of American local government should be re-examined in the light of this discussion. The emphasis in municipal reform movements on nonpartisanship in local government may be producing an unforeseen loss of public interest in local government. There is a profound internal inconsistency in the idea of nonpartisan local self-government.

In modern times a major struggle over the socialization of conflict has taken place in the field of labor relations. When President Theodore Roosevelt intervened in the coal strike in 1902, his action was regarded by many conservative newspaper editors as an "outrageous interference" in a private dispute.[5] On the other hand, the very words "union," "collective bargaining," "union recognition," "strike," "industrial unionism," and "industrywide bargaining" imply a tremendous socialization of a conflict which was once regarded as a purely private matter concerning only the employer and the individual workman.

The scope of the labor conflict is close to the essence of the controversy about collective bargaining: industrial and craft unionism, industrywide bargaining, sympathy strikes, union recognition and security, the closed shop, picketing, disclosure of information, political activity of unions, labor legislation, etc. All affect the scale of labor conflict. At every point the intervention of "outsiders," union organizers, federal and state agencies, courts, and police, has been disputed. The controversy has been to a very large degree about who can get into the fight and who is excluded.

Each side has had an adverse interest in the efforts of the other to extend the scale of its organization. Says Max Forester, "Lately, American employers have been showing a renewed interest in industrywide negotiations as a means of restoring a modicum of industry's 'lost power' at the bargaining table."[6]

The attempt to control the scope of conflict has a bearing on federal-state-local relations, for one way to restrict the scope of conflict is to *localize* it, while one way to expand it is to nationalize it. One of the most remarkable developments in recent American politics is the extent to which the federal, state, and local governments have become involved in *doing the same kinds of things* in large areas of public policy, so that it is possible for contestants to move freely from one level of government to another in an attempt to find the level at which they might try most advantageously to get what they want. This development has opened up vast new areas for the politics of scope. It follows that debates about federalism, local self-government, centralization, and decentralization are actually controversies about the scale of conflict.

In the case of a village of 1,000 within a state having a population of 3,500,000, a controversy lifted from the local to the state or the national level multiplies its scope by 3,500 or 180,000 times. Inevitably the outcome of a contest is controlled by the level at which the decision is made. What happens when the scope of conflict is multiplied by 180,000? (1) There is a great probability that the original contestants will lose control of the matter. (2) A host of new considerations and complications are introduced, and a multitude of new resources for a resolution of conflict becomes available; solutions inconceivable at a lower level may be worked out at a higher level.

The nationalization of politics inevitably breaks up old local power monopolies and old sectional power complexes; as a matter of fact, the new dimension produces so great a change in the scale of organization and the locus of power that it may take on a semirevolutionary character. The change of direction of party cleavages produced by the shift from sectional to national alignments has opened up a new political universe, a new order of possibilities and impossibilities.

Since 1920 the Negro population of the United States has increased by nearly five million, but nearly all of the increase has been in the northern states. There are now six northern states with a Negro population larger than the Negro population of Arkansas. These migrations have nationalized race relations and produced a new ratio of forces in the conflict over segregation and discrimination. The appeal for help in the conflict is from the 13 percent in the South to the 87 percent outside the South.

Everywhere the trends toward the privatization and socialization of conflict have been disguised as tendencies toward the centralization or decentralization, localization or nationalization of politics.

The question of scope is intrinsic in all concepts of political organization. The controversy about the nature and role of political parties and pressure groups, the relative merits of sectional and national party alignments, national party discipline, the locus of power in party organizations, the competitiveness of the party system, the way in which parties develop issues, and all attempts to democratize the internal processes of the parties are related to the scope of the political system.

The attack on politics, politicians, and political parties and the praise of nonpartisanship are significant in terms of the control of the scale of conflict. One-party systems, as an aspect of sharply sectional party alignments, have been notoriously useful instruments for the limitation of conflict and depression of political participation. This tends to be equally true of measures designed to set up nonpartisan government or measures designed to take important public business out of politics altogether.

The system of free private business enterprise is not merely a system of private ownership of property; it depends even more for its survival on the privacy of information about business transactions. It is probably true that the business system could not survive a full public disclosure of its internal transactions, because publicity would lead to the discovery and development of so many conflicts that large-scale public intervention would be inescapable.

To a great extent, the whole discussion of the role of government in modern society is at root a question of the scale conflict. *Democratic government is the greatest single instrument for the socialization of conflict in the American community.* The controversy about democracy might be interpreted in these terms also. Government in a democracy is a great engine for expanding the scale of conflict. Government is never far away when conflict breaks out. On the other hand, if the government lacks power or resources, vast numbers of potential conflicts cannot be developed because the community is unable to do anything about them. Therefore, government thrives on conflict. The work of the government has been aided and abetted by a host of public and private agencies and organizations designed to exploit every rift in the private world. Competitiveness is intensified by the legitimation of outside interference in private conflicts. It is necessary only to mention political parties, pressure groups, the courts, congressional investigations, governmental regulatory agencies, freedom of speech and press, among others, to show the range and variety of instruments available to the government for breaking open private conflicts. How does it happen that the government is the largest publisher in the country? Why is everything about public affairs vastly more newsworthy than business affairs are?

The scope of political conflict in the United States has been affected by the world crisis, which has fostered the development of a powerful national government operating on a global scale. Industrialization, urbanization, and nationalization have all but destroyed the meaning of the word "local" and have opened up great new areas of public interest and produced a new order of conflicts and alignments on an unprecedented scale. The visibility of conflict has been affected by the annihilation of space which has brought into view a new world. Universal suffrage, the most ambitious attempt to socialize conflict in American history, takes on a new meaning with the nationalization of politics and the development of a national electorate.

The development of American political institutions reflects the scale of their participation in conflict. The history of the United States Senate illustrates the way in which a public institution is affected by its widening involvement in national politics. In a series of decisions, the Senate first established the principle that individual senators are not bound by the instructions of state legislatures. Next, the direct popular election of senators has assimilated the Senate into the democratic system. It is noteworthy that the direct election of senators was followed shortly by the abolition of "executive" sessions. Today the Senate is a national institution; its survival as a major political institution has depended on its capacity to keep pace with the expanding political universe.

The history of the Presidency illustrates the same tendency. The rise of political parties and the extension of the suffrage produced the plebiscitary Presidency. The growth of presidential party leadership and the development of the Presidency as the political instrument of a national constituency have magnified the office tremendously. The Presidency has in turn become the principal instrument for the nationalization of politics.

The universalization of the franchise, the creation of a national electorate, and the development of the plebiscitary Presidency elected by a national constituency have facilitated the socialization of conflict. Thus, modern government has become the principal molder of the conflict system.

On the other hand, even in the public domain, extraordinary measures are taken occasionally to protect the internal processes of public agencies from publicity. Note the way in which the internal processes of the Supreme Court are handled, or the way diplomatic correspondence is shielded against public scrutiny, or the manner in which meetings of the President's cabinet are sealed off from the press, or the way in which the appearance of unanimity is used to check public intervention in the internal processes of the government at many critical points. Or note how Congress suppresses public information about its own internal expenditures. Everywhere privacy and publicity are potent implements of government.

The best point at which to manage conflict is before it starts. Once a conflict starts it is not easy to control because it is difficult to be exclusive about a fight. If one side is too hard-pressed, the impulse to redress the balance by inviting in outsiders is almost irresistible. Thus, the exclusion of the Negro from southern politics could be brought about only at the price of establishing a one-party system.

The expansion of the conflict may have consequences that are extremely distasteful to the original participants.[7] The tremendous growth of the Democratic Party after 1932 gave rise to a conflict between the old regular organizations and the newcomers. Why, for example, do the regular organizations prefer to take care of the new party workers in ad hoc organizations such as the Volunteers for Stevenson?

Other tensions within the Democratic party resulted from the increased political activity of labor unions, tensions between the old regular Democratic party organizations and the new political arm of the labor movement. On the other side, a factor in the lack of success of the Republican party in recent years seems to have been the reluctance of the old regular Republican party organizations to assimilate new party workers. At a time when tens of millions of Americans have developed a new interest in politics, the assimilation of newcomers into the old organizations has become a major problem, made difficult by the fact that every expansion of an association tends to reallocate power. Thus the very success of movements creates difficulties.

Is this not true of the labor movement also? Is it not likely that undemocratic procedures in labor unions are related to the attempt of old cadres to maintain control in the face of a great expansion of the membership? The growth of organizations is never an unmixed blessing to the individuals who first occupied the field. This seems to be true of all growing communities, rapidly expanding suburban communities for another example.

The dynamics of the expansion of the scope of conflict are something like this:

1. Competitiveness is the mechanism for the expansion of the scope of conflict. It is the *loser* who calls in outside help. (Jefferson, defeated within the Washington administration, went to the country for support.) The expansion of the electorate resulted from party competition for votes. As soon as it becomes likely that a new social group will get the vote, *both* parties favor the extension. *This is the expanding universe of politics.* On the other hand, any attempt to monopolize politics is almost by definition an attempt to limit the scope of conflict.

2. Visibility is a factor in the expanding of the scope of conflict. A democratic government lives by publicity. This proposition can be tested by examining the control of publicity in undemocratic regimes. Says Michael Lindsay about Communist China:

It is probably hard for the ordinary citizen of a democratic country to envisage the problem of obtaining reliable information about a totalitarian country. In democratic countries, especially in the United States, policy formation takes place with a good deal of publicity. When one turns to a totalitarian country, such as the Chinese People's Republic, the situation is completely different. All publications are controlled by the government and are avowedly propagandist. Criticism and discussion only appear when the government has decided to allow them. The process of policy formation is almost completely secret.[8]

3. The effectiveness of democratic government *as an instrument for the socialization of conflict depends on the amplitude of its powers and resources.* A powerful and re-

sourceful government is able to respond to conflict situations by providing an arena for them, publicizing them, protecting the contestants against retaliation, and taking steps to rectify the situations complained of; it may create new agencies to hear new categories of complaints and take special action about them.

Every social institution is affected by the way in which its internal processes are publicized. For example, the survival of the family as a social institution depends to a great extent on its privacy. It is almost impossible to imagine what forces in society might be released if all conflict in the private domain were thrown open for public exploitation. Procedures for the control of the expansive power of conflict determine the shape of the political system.

There is nothing intrinsically good or bad about any given scope of conflict. Whether a large conflict is better than a small conflict depends on what the conflict is about and what people want to accomplish. A change of scope makes possible a new pattern of competition, a new balance of forces, and a new result, but it also *makes impossible a lot of other things.*

While the language of politics is often oblique and sometimes devious, it is not difficult to show that the opposing tendencies toward the privatization and socialization of conflict underlie all strategy.

The study of politics calls for a sense of proportion; in the present case it requires a sense of the relative proportions of the belligerents and the spectators. At the outset of every political conflict the relations of the belligerents and the audience are so unstable that it is impossible to calculate the strength of the antagonists because all quantities in the equation are indeterminate until *all* of the bystanders have been committed.

Political conflict is not like a football game, played on a measured field by a fixed number of players in the presence of an audience scrupulously excluded from the playing field. Politics is much more like the original primitive game of football in which everybody was free to join, a game in which the whole population of one town might play the entire population of another town, moving freely back and forth across the countryside.

Many conflicts are narrowly confined by a variety of devices, but the distinctive quality of political conflicts is that the relations between the players and the audience have not been well defined and there is usually nothing to keep the audience from getting into the game.

Notes

1. "The indirect approach is as fundamental to the realm of politics as to that of sex." Liddell Hart, quoted by Al Newman in *The Reporter,* October 15, 1958, p. 45.

2. John Dollard, *Caste and Class in a Southern Town,* 3d ed., Doubleday and Company, Garden City, 1957, p. 72. See also pp. 208–211 for a discussion of bipartisan arrangements in the South to depress conflict. Dollard discusses the impact of the one-party system on voting participation. Often the argument is made that the Negro *would be contented if left alone by outsiders.*

3. Vidich and Bensman, *Small Town in Mass Society,* Princeton, 1958. Members of the board resort to "inchoately arrived-at unanimous decisions in which no vote, or only a perfunctory one, is taken." They "attempt to minimize or avoid crises, and this leads to further demands for unanimity and concealment." pp. 172–173.

"There is always the danger that, should an issue come into the open, conflicting parties will appeal to outside individuals or groups or to more important figures in the machine. Public sentiment could easily be mobilized around the issues." p. 127.

"In the ordinary conduct of business in this manner, issues and conflict never become visible at the public level. Undisciplined appeals to outside groups which would threaten the monopoly of power of the controlling group do not occur." p. 128. See also p. 133.

4. Lansing (Michigan) *State Journal,* July 15, 1958. The statement was made in response to a challenge following an election contest.

5. See Frederick Lewis Allen, *The Great Pierpont Morgan,* Bantam Biography, New York, 1956, pp. 175–177.

6. *New York Herald Tribune,* February 1, 1959.

See also statements by George Romney, president of American Motors Corporation, *Wall Street Journal,* January 21 and February 2, 1959.

7. A classical case is described by John F. Fairbank ("Formosa through China's Eyes," *New Republic,* October 13, 1958), in terms of Chinese military and diplomatic history. "Contenders for power in traditional China commonly found it essential to utilize the barbarians, for the latter were powerful fighters, though often naïve in politics and easily swayed by their feelings of pride and fear. There is a great body of lore and precedent on this subject in Chinese historical annals. Sometimes the Chinese were out-manipulated by the barbarians. The Sung Emperors, for example, made a mistake in getting Mongol help against the Jurchen invaders from Manchuria; the Mongols eventually conquered China. Similarly the Manchus stayed to conquer and rule the country."

8. *New York Times Magazine,* "The Chinese Puzzle: Mao's Foreign Policy," October 12, 1958.

2

The Scope and Bias
of the Pressure System

THE scope of conflict is an aspect of the scale of political organization and the extent of political competition. The size of the constituencies being mobilized, the inclusiveness or exclusiveness of the conflicts people expect to develop have a bearing on all theories about how politics is or should be organized. In other words, nearly all theories about politics have something to do with the question of who can get into the fight and who is to be excluded.

Every regime is a testing ground for theories of this sort. More than any other system American politics provides the raw materials for testing the organizational assumptions of two contrasting kinds of politics, *pressure politics* and *party politics*.[1] The concepts that underlie these forms of politics constitute the raw stuff of a general theory of political action. The basic issue between the two patterns of organization is one of size and scope of conflict; pressure groups are small-scale organizations while political parties are very large-scale organizations. One need not be surprised, therefore, that the partisans of large-scale and small-scale organizations differ passionately, because the outcome of the political game depends on the scale on which it is played.

To understand the controversy about the scale of political organization it is necessary first to take a look at some theories about interest-group politics. Pressure groups have played a remarkable role in American politics, but they have played an even more remarkable role in American political theory. Considering the political condition of the country in the first third of the twentieth century, it was probably inevitable that the discussion of special-interest pressure groups should lead to development of "group" theories of politics in which an attempt is made to explain everything in terms of group activity, i.e., an attempt to formulate a universal group theory. Since one of the best ways to test an idea is to ride it into the ground, political theory has unquestionably been improved by the heroic attempt to create a political universe revolving about the group. Now that we have a number of drastic statements of the group theory of politics pushed to a great extreme, we ought to be able to see what the limitations of the idea are.

Political conditions in the first third of the present century were extremely hospitable to the idea. The role of business in the strongly sectional Republican system from 1896 to 1932 made the dictatorship of business seem to be a part of the eternal order of things. Moreover, the regime as a whole seemed to be so stable that questions about the survival of the American community did not arise. The general interests of the community were easily overlooked under these circumstances.

Nevertheless, in spite of the excellent and provocative scholarly work done by Beard, Latham, Truman, Leiserson, Dahl, Lindblom, Laski, and others, the group theory of politics is beset with difficulties. The difficulties are theoretical, growing in part out of sheer overstatements of the idea and in part out of some confusion about the nature of modern government.

One difficulty running through the literature of the subject results from the attempt to explain *everything* in terms of the group theory.[2] On general grounds it would be remarkable indeed if a single hypothesis explained everything about so complex a subject as American politics. Other difficulties have grown out of the fact that group concepts have been stated in terms so universal that the subject seems to have no shape or form.

The question is: Are pressure groups the universal basic ingredient of all political situations, and do they explain everything? To answer this question it is necessary to review a bit of rudimentary political theory.

Two modest reservations might be made merely to test the group dogma. We might clarify our ideas if (1) we explore more fully the possibility of making a distinction between public-interest groups and special-interest groups and (2) if we distinguished between organized and unorganized groups. These reservations do not disturb the main body of group theory, but they may be useful when we attempt to define general propositions more precisely. If both of these distinctions can be validated, we may get hold of something that has scope and limits and is capable of being defined. The awkwardness of a discussion of political phenomena in terms of universals is that the subject has no beginning or end; it is impossible to distinguish one subject from another or to detect the bias of the forces involved because scope and bias are aspects of limitations of the subject. It cannot really be said that we have seen a subject until we have seen its outer limits and thus are able to draw a line between one subject and another.

We might begin to break the problem into its component parts by exploring the distinction between public and private interests.[3] If we can validate this distinction, we shall have established one of the boundaries of the subject.

As a matter of fact, the distinction between *public* and *private* interests is a thoroughly respectable one; it is one of the oldest known to political theory. In the literature of the subject, the public interest refers to general or common interests shared by all or by substantially all members of the community.[4] Presumably no community exists unless there is some kind of community of interests, just as there is no nation without some notion of national interests. If it is really impossible to distinguish between private and public interests, the group theorists have produced a revolution in political thought so great that it is impossible to foresee its consequences. For this reason the distinction ought to be explored with great care.

At a time when nationalism is described as one of the most dynamic forces in the world, it should not be difficult to understand that national interests actually do exist.[5] It is necessary only to consider the proportion of the American budget devoted to national defense to realize that the common interest in national survival is a great one. Measured in dollars this interest is one of the biggest things in the world. Moreover, it is difficult to describe this interest as special. The diet on which the American leviathan feeds is something more than a jungle of disparate special interests. In the literature of democratic theory the body of common agreement found in the community is known as the "consensus," without which it is believed that no democratic system can survive.

The reality of the common interest is suggested by demonstrated capacity of the community to survive. There must be something that holds people together.

In contrast with the common interests are the special interests. The implication of this term is that these are interests shared by only a few people or a fraction of the community; they *exclude* others and may be *adverse* to them. A special interest is exclusive in about the same way as private property is exclusive. In a complex society it is not surprising that there are some interests that are shared by all or substantially all members of the community and some interests that are not shared so widely. The distinction is useful precisely because conflicting claims are made by people about the nature of their interests in controversial matters.

Perfect agreement within the community is not always possible, but an interest may be said to have become public when it is shared so widely as to be substantially universal. Thus, the difference between 99 percent agreement and perfect agreement is not so great that it becomes necessary to argue that all interests are special, that the interests of the 99 percent are as special as the interests of the 1 percent. For example, the law is probably doing an adequate job of defining the public interest in domestic tranquility despite the fact that there is nearly always one dissenter at every hanging. That is, the law defines the public interest in spite of the fact that there may be some outlaws.

Since one function of theory is to explain reality, it is reasonable to add that it is a good deal easier to explain what is going on in politics by making a distinction between public and private interests than it is to attempt to explain *everything* in terms of special interests. The attempt to prove that all interests are special forces us into circumlocutions such as those involved in the argument that people have special interests in the common good. The argument can be made, but it seems a long way around to avoid a useful distinction.

What is to be said about the argument that the distinction between public and special interests is "subjective" and is therefore "unscientific"?

All discussion of interests, special as well as general, refers to the motives, desires, and intentions of people. In this sense the whole discussion of interests is subjective. We have made progress in the study of politics because people have observed some kind of relation between the political behavior of people and certain wholly impersonal data concerning their ownership of property, income, economic status, professions, and the like. All that we know about interests, private as well as public, is based on inferences of this sort. Whether the distinction in any given case is valid depends on the evidence and on the kinds of inferences drawn from the evidence.

The only meaningful way we can speak of the interests of an association like the National Association of Manufacturers is to draw inferences from the fact that the membership is a select group to which only manufacturers may belong and to try to relate that datum to what the association does. The implications, logic, and deductions are persuasive only if they furnish reasonable explanations of the facts. That is all that any theory about interests can do. It has seemed persuasive to students of politics to suppose that manufacturers do not join an association to which only manufacturers may belong merely to promote philanthropic or cultural or religious interests, for example. The basis of selection of the membership creates an inference about the organization's concerns. The conclusions drawn from this datum seem to fit what we know about the policies promoted by the association; i.e., the policies seem to reflect the exclusive interests of manufacturers. The method is not foolproof, but it works better than many other kinds of analysis and is useful precisely because special-interest groups often tend to rationalize their special interests as public interests.

Is it possible to distinguish between the "interests" of the members of the National Association of Manufacturers and the members of the American League to Abolish Capital Punishment? The facts in the two cases are not identical. First, *the members of the A.L.A.C.P. obviously do not expect to be hanged.* The membership of the A.L.A.C.P. is not restricted to persons under indictment for murder or in jeopardy of the extreme penalty. *Anybody* can join A.L.A.C.P. Its members oppose capital punishment, although they are not personally likely to benefit by the policy they advocate. The inference is therefore that the interest of the A.L.A.C.P. is not adverse, exclusive, or special. It is not like the interest of the Petroleum Institute in depletion allowances.

Take some other cases. The members of the National Child Labor Committee are not children in need of legislative protection against exploitation by employers. The members of the World Peace Foundation apparently want peace, but in the nature of things they must want peace for everyone because no group can be at peace while the rest of the community is at war. Similarly, even if the members of the National Defense League wanted defense only for themselves, they would necessarily have to work for defense for the whole country because national security is indivisible. Only a naive person is likely to imagine that the political involvements of the members of the American Bankers Association and members of the Foreign Policy Association are identical. In other words, we may draw inferences from the exclusive or the nonexclusive nature of benefits sought by organizations as well as we can from the composition of groups. The positions of these groups can be distinguished not on the basis of some subjective process, but by making reasonable inferences from verifiable facts.

On the other hand, because some special-interest groups attempt to identify themselves with the public interest it does not follow that the whole idea of the public interest is a fraud. Mr. Wilson's famous remark that what is good for General Motors is good for the country assumes that people generally do in fact desire the common good. Presumably, Mr. Wilson attempted to explain the special interest of General Motors in terms of the common interest because that was the only way he could talk to people who do not belong to the General Motors organization. *Within* the General Motors organization, discussions might be carried on in terms of naked self-interest, but a *public discussion must be carried on in public terms.*

All public discussion is addressed to the general community. To describe the conflict of special-interest groups as a form of politics means that the conflict has become generalized, has become a matter involving the broader public. In the nature of things *a political conflict among special interests is never restricted to the group most immediately interested.* Instead, it is an appeal (initiated by relatively small numbers of people) for the support of vast numbers of people who are sufficiently remote to have a somewhat different perspective on the controversy. It follows that Mr. Wilson's comment, far from demonstrating that the public interest is a fraud, proves that he thinks that the public interest is so important that even a great private corporation must make obeisance to it.

The distinction between public and special interests is an indispensable tool for the study of politics. To abolish the distinction is to make a shambles of political science by treating things that are different as if they were alike. The kind of distinction made here is a commonplace of all literature dealing with human society, but *if we accept it, we have established one of the outer limits of the subject;* we have split the world of interests in half and have taken one step toward defining the scope of this kind of political conflict.

We can now examine the second distinction, the distinction between organized and unorganized groups. The question here is not whether the distinction can be made but whether or not it is worth making. Organization has been described as "merely a stage or degree of interaction" in the development of a group.[6]

The proposition is a good one, but what conclusions do we draw from it? We do not dispose of the matter by calling the distinction between organized and unorganized groups a "mere" difference of degree because some of the greatest differences in the world are differences of degree. As far as special-interest politics is concerned the implication to be avoided is that a few workmen who habitually stop at a corner saloon for a glass of beer are essentially the same as the United States Army because the difference between them is merely one of degree. At this point we have distinction that makes a difference. The distinction between organized and unorganized groups is worth making because it ought to alert us against an analysis which begins as a general group theory of politics but ends with a defense of pressure politics as inherent, universal, permanent, and inevitable. This kind of confusion comes from the loosening of categories involved in the universalization of group concepts.

Since the beginning of intellectual history, scholars have sought to make progress in their work by distinguishing between things that are unlike and by dividing their subject matter into categories to examine them more intelligently. It is something of a novelty, therefore, when group theorists reverse this process by discussing their subject in terms so universal that they wipe out all categories, because this is the dimension in which it is least possible to understand anything.

If we are able, therefore, to distinguish between public and private interests and between organized and unorganized groups we have marked out the major boundaries of the subject; *we have given the subject shape and scope.* We are now in a position to attempt to define the area we want to explore. Having cut the pie into four pieces, we can now appropriate the piece we want and leave the rest to someone else. For a multitude of reasons *the most likely field of study is that of the organized, special-interest groups.* The advantage of concentrating on organized groups is that they are known, identifiable, and recognizable. The advantage of concentrating on special-interest groups is that they have one important characteristic in common; they are all exclusive. This piece of the pie (the organized special-interest groups) we shall call the *pressure system.* The pressure system has boundaries we can define; we can fix its scope and make an attempt to estimate its bias.

It may be assumed at the outset that all organized special-interest groups have some kind of impact on politics. A sample survey of organizations made by the Trade Associations Division of the United States Department of Commerce in 1942 concluded that "From 70 to 100 percent (of these associations) are planning activities in the field of government relations, trade promotion, trade practices, public relations, annual conventions, cooperation with other organizations, and information services."[7]

The subject of our analysis can be reduced to manageable proportions and brought under control if we restrict ourselves to the groups whose interests in politics are sufficient to have led them to unite in formal organizations having memberships, bylaws, and officers. A further advantage of this kind of definition is, we may assume, that the organized special-interest groups are the most self-conscious, best developed, most intense and active groups. Whatever claims can be made for a group theory of politics ought to be sustained by the evidence concerning these groups, if the claims have any validity at all.

The organized groups listed in the various directories (such as *National Associations of the United States,* published at intervals by the United States Department of Commerce) and specialty yearbooks, registers, etc. and the *Lobby Index*, published by the United States House of Representatives, probably include the bulk of the organizations in the pressure system. All compilations are incomplete, but these are extensive enough to provide us with some basis for estimating the scope of the system.

By the time a group has developed the kind of interest that leads it to organize, it may be assumed that it has also developed some kind of political bias because *organization is itself a mobilization of bias in preparation for action.* Since these groups can be identified and since they have memberships (i.e., they include and exclude people), it is possible to think of the *scope* of the system.

When lists of these organizations are examined, the fact that strikes the student most forcibly is that *the system is very small.* The range of organized, identifiable, known groups is amazingly narrow; there is nothing remotely universal about it. There is a tendency on the part of the publishers of directories of associations to place an undue emphasis on business organizations, an emphasis that is almost inevitable because the business community is by a wide margin the most highly organized segment of society. Publishers doubtless tend also to reflect public demand for information. Nevertheless, the dominance of business groups in the pressure system is so marked that it probably cannot be explained away as an accident of the publishing industry.

The business character of the pressure system is shown by almost every list available. *National Associations of the United States*[8] lists 1,860 business associations out of a total of 4,000 in the volume, though it refers without listing (p. VII) to 16,000 organizations of businessmen. One cannot be certain what the total content of the unknown associational universe may be, but, taken with the evidence found in other compilations, it is obvious that business is remarkably well represented. Some evidence of the over-all scope of the system is to be seen in the estimate that 15,000 national trade associations have a gross membership of about one million business firms.[9] The data are incomplete, but even if we do not have a detailed map this is the shore dimly seen.

Much more directly related to pressure politics is the *Lobby Index, 1946–1949* (an index of organizations and individuals registering or filing quarterly reports under the Federal Lobbying Act), published as a report of the House Select Committee on Lobbying Activities. In this compilation, 825 out of a total of 1,247 entries (exclusive of individuals and Indian tribes) represented business.[10] A selected list of the most important of the groups listed in the *Index* (the groups spending the largest sums of money on lobbying) published in the *Congressional Quarterly Log* shows 149 business organizations in a total of 265 listed.[11]

The business or upper-class bias of the pressure system shows up everywhere. Businessmen are four or five times as likely to write to their congressmen as manual laborers are. College graduates are far more apt to write to their congressmen than people in the lowest educational category are.[12]

The limited scope of the business pressure system is indicated by all available statistics. Among business organizations, the National Association of Manufacturers (with about 20,000 corporate members) and the Chamber of Commerce of the United States (about as large as the N.A.M.) are giants. Usually business associations are much smaller. Of 421 trade associations in the metal-products industry listed in *National Associations of the United States,* 153 have a membership of less than 20.[13] The median membership was somewhere between 24 and 50. Approximately the same scale of memberships is to be found in the lumber, furniture, and paper industries where 37.3 percent of the associations listed had a membership of less than 20 and the median membership was in the 25 to 50 range.[14]

The statistics in these cases are representative of nearly all other classifications of industry.

Data drawn from other sources support this thesis. Broadly, the pressure system has an upper-class bias. There is overwhelming evidence that participation in voluntary organizations is related to upper social and economic status; the rate of participation is much higher in the upper strata than it is elsewhere. The general proposition is well stated by Lazarsfeld:

People on the lower SES levels are less likely to belong to any organizations than the people on high SES (Social and Economic Status) levels. (On an A and B level, we find 72 percent of these respondents who belong to one or more organizations. The proportion of respondents who are members of formal organizations decreases steadily as SES level descends until, on the D level only 35 percent of the respondents belong to any associations).[15]

The bias of the system is shown by the fact that *even nonbusiness organizations reflect an upper-class tendency.*

Lazarsfeld's generalization seems to apply equally well to urban and rural populations. The obverse side of the coin is that large areas of the population appear to be wholly outside the system of private organization. A study made by Ira Reid of a Philadelphia area showed that in a sample of 963 persons, 85 percent belonged to no civic or charitable organization and 74 percent belonged to no occupational, business, or professional associations, while another Philadelphia study of 1,154 women showed that 55 percent belonged to no associations of any kind.[16]

A *Fortune* farm poll taken some years ago found that 70.5 percent of farmers belonged to no agricultural organizations. A similar conclusion was reached by two Gallup polls showing that perhaps no more than one third of the farmers of the country belonged to farm organizations,[17] while another *Fortune* poll showed that 86.8 percent of the low-income farmers belonged to no farm organizations.[18] All available data support the generalization that the farmers who do not participate in rural organizations are largely the poorer ones.

A substantial amount of research done by other rural sociologists points to the same conclusion. Mangus and Cottam say, on the basis of a study of 556 heads of Ohio farm families and their wives:

The present study indicates that comparatively few of those who ranked low on the scale of living took any active part in community organizations as members, attendants, contributors, or leaders. On the other hand, those families that ranked high on the scale of living comprised the vast majority of the highly active participants in formal group activities. . . . Fully two-thirds of those in the lower class as defined in this study were non-participants as compared with only one-tenth of those in the upper class and one-fourth of those in the middle class. . . . When families were classified by the general level-of-living index, 16 times as large a proportion of those in the upper classes as of those in the lower class were active participants. . . .[19]

Along the same line Richardson and Bauder observe, "Socio-economic status was directly related to participation."[20] In still another study it was found that "a highly significant relationship existed between income and formal participation."[21] It was found that persons with more than four years of college education held twenty times as many memberships (per one hundred persons) as did those with less than a fourth-grade education and were forty times as likely to hold office in nonchurch organizations, while persons with an income over $5,000 hold ninety-four times as many offices as persons with incomes less than $250.[22]

D.E. Lindstrom found that 72 percent of farm laborers belonged to no organizations whatever.[23]

There is a great wealth of data supporting the proposition that participation in private associations exhibits a class bias.[24]

The class bias of associational activity gives meaning to the limited scope of the pressure system, because *scope and bias are aspects of the same tendency.* The data raise a serious question about the validity of the proposition that special-interest groups are a universal form of political organization reflecting *all* interests. As a matter of fact, to suppose that everyone participates in pressure-group activity and that all interests get themselves organized in the pressure system is to destroy the meaning of this form of politics. The pressure system makes sense only as the political instrument of a segment of the community. It gets results by being selective and biased; *if everybody got into the act, the unique advantages of this form of organization would be destroyed, for it is possible that if all interests could be mobilized the result would be a stalemate.*

Special-interest organizations are most easily formed when they deal with small numbers of individuals who are acutely aware of their exclusive interests. To describe the conditions of presssure-group organization in this way is, however, to say that it is primarily a business phenomenon. Aside from a few very large organizations (the churches, organized labor, farm organizations, and veterans' organizations) the residue is a small segment of the population. *Pressure politics is essentially the politics of small groups.*

The vice of the groupist theory is that it conceals the most significant aspects of the system. The flaw in the pluralist heaven is that the heavenly chorus sings with a strong upper-class accent. Probably about 90 percent of the people cannot get into the pressure system.

The notion that the pressure system is automatically representative of the whole community is a myth fostered by the universalizing tendency of modern group theories. *Pressure politics is a selective process* ill designed to serve diffuse interests. The system is skewed, loaded, and unbalanced in favor of a fraction of a minority.

On the other hand, pressure tactics are not remarkably successful in mobilizing general interests. When pressure-group organizations attempt to represent the interests of large numbers of people, they are usually able to reach only a small segment of their constituencies. Only a chemical trace of the fifteen million Negroes in the United States belong to the National Association for the Advancement of Colored People. Only one five hundredths of 1 percent of American women belong to the League of Women Voters, only one sixteen hundredths of 1 percent of the consumers belong to the National Consumers' League, and only 6 percent of American automobile drivers belong to the American Automobile Association, while about 15 percent of the veterans belong to the American Legion.

The competing claims of pressure groups and political parties for the loyalty of the American public revolve about the difference between the results likely to be achieved by small-scale and large-scale political organization. Inevitably, the outcome of pressure politics and party politics will be vastly different.

A Critique of Group Theories of Politics

It is extremely unlikely that the vogue of group theories of politics would have attained its present status if its basic assumptions had not been first established by some concept of economic determinism. The economic interpretation of politics has always appealed to those political philosophers who have sought a single prime mover, a sort of philosopher's stone of political science around which to organize their ideas. The search for a single, ultimate cause has something to do with the attempt to explain *everything* about politics in terms of group concepts. The logic of economic determinism is to *identify the origins of conflict and to assume the conclusion.* This kind of thought has some of the earmarks of an illusion. The somnambulatory quality of thinking in this field appears also in the tendency of research to deal only with successful pressure campaigns or the willingness of scholars to be satisfied with having placed pressure groups on the scene of the crime without following through to see if the effect can really be attributed to the cause. What makes this kind of thinking remarkable is the fact that in political contests there are as many failures as there are successes. Where in the literature of pressure politics are the failures?

Students of special-interest politics need a more sophisticated set of intellectual tools than they have developed thus far. The theoretical problem involved in the search for a single cause is that all power relations in a democracy are reciprocal. Trying to find the original cause is like trying to find the first wave of the ocean.

Can we really assume that we know all that is to be known about a conflict if we understand its *origins?* Everything we know about politics suggests that a conflict is likely to change profoundly as it becomes political. It is a rare individual who can confront his antagonists without changing his opinions to some degree. Everything changes once a conflict gets into the political arena—*who* is involved, *what* the conflict is about, the resources available, etc. It is extremely difficult to predict the outcome of a fight by watching its beginning because we do not even know who else is going to get into the conflict. The logical consequence of the exclusive emphasis on the determinism of the private origins of conflict is to assign zero value to the political process.

The very expression "pressure politics" invites us to misconceive the role of special-interest groups in politics. The word "pressure" implies the use of some kind of force, a form of intimidation, something other than reason and information, to induce public authorities to act against their own best judgment. In Latham's famous statement already quoted the legislature is described as a "referee" who "ratifies" and "records" the "balance of power" among the contending groups.[25]

It is hard to imagine a more effective way of saying that Congress has no mind or force of its own or that Congress is unable to invoke new forces that might alter the equation.

Actually the outcome of political conflict is not like the "resultant" of opposing forces in physics. To assume that the forces in a political situation could be diagramed as a physicist might diagram the resultant of opposing physical forces is to wipe the slate clean of all remote, general, and public considerations for the protection of which civil societies have been instituted.

Moreover, the notion of "pressure" distorts the image of the power relations involved. *Private conflicts are taken into the public arena precisely because someone wants to make certain that the power ratio among the private interests most immediately involved shall not prevail*. To treat a conflict as a mere test of the strength of the private interests is to leave out the most significant factors. This is so true that it might indeed be said that the only way to preserve private power ratios is to keep conflicts out of the public arena.

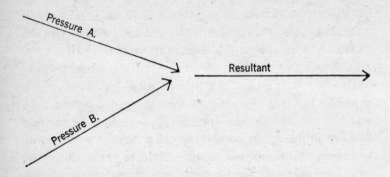

The assumption that it is only the "interested" who count ought to be re-examined in view of the foregoing discussion. The tendency of the literature of pressure politics has been to neglect the low-tension force of large numbers because it *assumes that the equation of forces is fixed at the outset.*

Given the assumptions made by the group theorists, the attack on the idea of the majority is completely logical. The assumption is that conflict is monopolized narrowly by the parties immediately concerned. There is no room for a majority when conflict is defined so narrowly. It is a great deficiency of the group theory that it has found no place in the political system for the majority. The force of the majority is of an entirely different order of magnitude, something not to be measured by pressure-group standards.

Instead of attempting to exterminate all political forms, organizations, and alignments that do not qualify as pressure groups, would it not be better to attempt to make a synthesis, covering the whole political system and finding a place for all kinds of political life?

One possible synthesis of pressure politics and party politics might be produced by *describing politics as the socialization of conflict*. That is to say, the political process is a sequence: conflicts are initiated by highly motivated, high-tension groups so directly and immediately involved that it is difficult for them to see the justice of competing claims. As long as the conflicts of these groups remain *private* (carried on in terms of economic competition, reciprocal denial of goods and services, private negotiations and bargaining, struggles for corporate control or competition for membership), no political process is initiated. Conflicts become political only when an attempt is made to involve the wider public. Pressure politics might be described as a stage in the socialization of conflict. This analysis makes pressure politics an integral part of all politics, including party politics.

One of the characteristic points of origin of pressure politics is a breakdown of the discipline of the business community. The flight to government is perpetual. Something like this is likely to happen wherever there is a point of contact between competing power systems. It is the *losers in intra-business conflict who seek redress from public authority. The dominant business interests resist appeals to the government.* The role of the government as the patron of the defeated private interest sheds light on its function as the critic of private power relations.

Since the contestants in private conflicts are apt to be unequal in strength, it follows that *the most powerful special interests want private settlements* because they are able to dictate the outcome as long as the conflict remains private. If A is a hundred times as strong as B he does not welcome the intervention of a third party because he expects to impose his own terms on B; he wants to isolate B. He is especially opposed to the intervention of public authority, because public authority represents the most overwhelming form of outside intervention. Thus, if $\dfrac{A}{B} = \dfrac{100}{1}$, it is obviously not to A's advantage to involve a third party a million times as strong as A and B combined. Therefore, it is the weak, not the strong, who appeal to public authority for relief. It is the weak who want to socialize conflict, i.e., to involve more and more people in the conflict until the balance of forces is changed. In the schoolyard it is not the bully but the defenseless smaller boys who "tell the teacher." When the teacher intervenes, the balance of power in the schoolyard is apt to change drastically. It is the function of public authority to *modify private power relations by enlarging the scope of conflict.* Nothing could be more mistaken than to suppose that public authority merely registers the dominance of the strong over the weak. The mere existence of public order has already ruled out a great variety of forms of private pressure. Nothing could be more confusing than to suppose that the refugees from the business community who come to Congress for relief and protection *force* Congress to do their bidding.

Evidence of the truth of this analysis may be seen in the fact that the big private interests do not necessarily win if they are involved in public conflicts with petty interests. The image of the lobbyists as primarily the agents of big business is not easy to support on the face of the record of congressional hearings, for example. The biggest corporations in the country tend to avoid the arena in which pressure groups and lobbyists fight it out before congressional committees. To describe this process exclusively in terms of an effort of business to intimidate congressmen is to misconceive what is actually going on.

It is probably a mistake to assume that pressure politics is the typical or even the most important relation between government and business. The pressure group is by no means the perfect instrument of the business community.

What does big business want? The *winners* in intrabusiness strife want (1) to be let alone (they want autonomy) and (2) to preserve the solidarity of the business community. For these purposes pressure politics is not a wholly satisfactory device. The most elementary considerations of strategy call for the business community to develop some kind of common policy more broadly based than any special-interest group is likely to be.

The political influence of business depends on the kind of solidarity that, on the one hand, leads all business to rally to the support of *any* businessman in trouble with the government and, on the other hand, keeps internal business disputes out of the public arena. In this system businessmen resist the impulse to attack each other in public and discourage the efforts of individual members of the business community to take intrabusiness conflicts into politics.

The attempt to mobilize a united front of the whole business community does not resemble the classical concept of pressure politics. The logic of business politics is to keep peace within the business community by supporting as far as possible all claims that business groups make for themselves. The tendency is to support all businessmen who have conflicts with the government and support all businessmen in conflict with labor. In this way *special-interest politics can be converted into party policy*. The search is for a broad base of political mobilization grounded on the strategic need for political organization on a wider scale than is possible in the case of the historical pressure group. Once the business community begins to think in terms of a larger scale of political organization the Republican party looms large in business politics.

It is a great achievement of American democracy that business has been forced to form a political organization designed to win elections, i.e., has been forced to compete for power in the widest arena in the political system. On the other hand, *the power of the Republican party to make terms with business rests on the fact that business cannot afford to be isolated.*

The Republican party has played a major role in *the political organization of the business community,* a far greater role than many students of politics seem to have realized. The influence of business in the Republican party is great, but it is never absolute because business is remarkably dependent on the party. The business community is too small, it arouses too much antagonism, and its aims are too narrow to win the support of a popular majority. The political education of business is a function of the Republican party that can never be done so well by anyone else.

In the management of the political relations of the business community, the Republican party is much more important than any combination of pressure groups ever could be. The success of special interests in Congress is due less to the "pressure" exerted by these groups than it is due to the fact that Republican members of Congress are committed in advance to a general probusiness attitude. The notion that business groups coerce Republican congressmen into voting for their bills underestimates the whole Republican posture in American politics.[26]

It is not easy to manage the political interests of the business community because there is a perpetual stream of losers in intrabusiness conflicts who go to the government for relief and protection. It has not been possible therefore to maintain perfect solidarity, and when solidarity is breached the government is involved almost automatically. The fact that business has not become hopelessly divided and that it has retained great influence in American politics has been due chiefly to the over-all mediating role played by the Republican party. There has never been a pressure group or a combination of pressure groups capable of performing this function.

Notes

1. Pressure groups have been defined by V. O. Key as "private associations . . . (which) promote their interests by attempting to influence government rather than by nominating candidates and seeking responsibility for the management of government," *Politics, Parties, and Pressure Groups*, 4th ed., New York, 1958, p. 23.

On the other hand, political parties try to get general control of the government by electing their candidates to the most important public offices.

2. Earl Latham, *The Group Basis of Politics*, Ithaca, 1952, pp. 35 and 36, says, "The legislature referees the group struggle, ratifies the victories of the successful coalitions, and records the terms of the surrenders, compromises, and conquests in the form of statutes. . . ." "the legislative vote on which any issue tends to represent the composition of strength, i.e., the balance of power, among the contending groups at the moment of voting."

3. The discussion here refers generally to the analysis made by David Truman in his distinguished volume *The Government Process*, New York, 1951. See especially pp. 50–51, 65.

4. References to the public interest appear under a variety of headings in the literature of political theory.

See G. D. H. Cole's comment on "the will of all" and the "general will," pp. xxx and xxxi of his introduction to Everyman's edition of Rousseau's *Social Contract*, London, 1913.

See Ernst Cassirer, *The Myth of the State*, Garden City, 1955, pp. 88–93, for a discussion of Plato's concept of "justice" as the end of the state in his criticism of the sophists.

See S. D. Lindsay, *The Essentials of Democracy*, Philadelphia 1929, p. 49, for a statement regarding consensus.

5. It does not seem necessary to argue that nationalism and national interests are forces in the modern world. E. H. Carr writes about "the catastrophic growth of nationalism" in *Nationalism and After*, New York, 1945, p. 18. D. W. Brogan describes nations as "the only communities that now exist," *The American Character*, New York, 1944, p. 169. "The outstanding and distinctive characteristic of the people of the Western States System is their devotion and allegiance to the 'nations' into which they have got themselves divided," Frederick L. Schumann, *International Politics*, 3d ed., New York, 1941, p. 300. A. D. Lindsay in *The Essentials of Democracy*, Philadelphia, 1929, p. 49, has stated the doctrine of the democratic consensus as follows: "Nationality, however produced, is a sense of belonging together, involving a readiness on the part of the members of a state to subordinate their differences to it. It involves something more. It has a connection with the notion of a distinctive culture—some sort of

rough ideal of the kind of common life for which the community stands, which always exists in people's minds as a rough criticism by which political proposals are to be judged. This at least is clear, that where such common understanding and sense of belonging together either does not exist or is overshadowed by other differences, successful democracy is not really possible."

6. Truman, *op. cit.*, p. 51.

7. *National Associations of the United States*, p. xi.

8. Edited by Jay Judkins, Washington, 1949, p. viii.

9. *National Associations of the United States*, p. viii.

10. House Report No. 3197, 81st Congress, 2d Session, December 15, 1950, Washington.

11. *Congressional Quarterly Log*, week ending February 24, 1950, pp. 217 ff. Another compilation, the list of approximately one thousand associations and societies published in the *World Almanac* for 1953, reflects to a very great extent the economic, professional and leisure interests and activities of the upper economic strata of the community. Scarcely more than a dozen or so of the associations listed in the *World Almanac* can be described as proletarian in their outlook or membership.

12. *American Institute of Public Opinion*, May 29, 1946.

13. Four hundred fifty associations are listed, but figures for membership are given for only 421.

14. Membership statistics are given for only 177 of the 200 associations listed.

15. Lazarsfeld and Associates, *The People's Choice*, p. 145.

16. Reid and Ehle, "Leadership Selection in the Urban Locality Areas," *Public Opinion Quarterly* (1950), 14:262–284. See also Powell, *Anatomy of Public Opinion*, New York, 1951, pp. 180–181.

17. See Carey McWilliams, *Small Farm and Big Farm*, Public Affairs Pamphlet, No. 100.

18. *Fortune* poll, April, 1943.

19. A. R. Mangus and H. R. Cottam, *Level of Living, Social Participation, and Adjustment of Ohio Farm People*, Ohio Agricultural Experiment Station, Wooster, Ohio, Bull. 624, September, 1941, pp. 51, 53.

Another study (of New York farmers) shows that there is a direct relation between organizational activity and the economic status of farmers. The author concludes that "the operators of farms of less than 55 acres in size are represented in only very small proportions in membership in the farm bureau and in the Dairymen's League and other cooperatives." W. A. Anderson, *The Membership of Farmers in New York Organizations*, Cornell University Agricultural Experiment Station, Ithaca, N.Y., 1937, p. 20.

20. P. D. Richardson and Ward W. Bauder, *Participation in Organized Activities in a Kentucky Rural Community*. Kentucky Agricultural Experimental Station, University of Kentucky, Bulletin 598, 1953, Lexington, Kentucky, pp. 26, 28. "The number of memberships varied directly with the socio-economic score."

21. Harold F. Kaufman, *Participation in Organized Activities in Selected Kentucky Localities*, Bulletin 528, Kentucky Agricultural Experiment Station, University of Kentucky, Lexington, 1949, p. 19.

22. *Ibid.*, pp. 11, 12, 13, 21.

See also Mirra Komorovsky, "The Voluntary Association of Urban Dwellers," *American Sociological Review*, 11:686–98, 1946.

23. *Forces Affecting Participation of Farm People in Rural Organizations*, University of Illinois Agricultural Experiment Station, Bulletin 423, 1936, p. 103.

24. "Associational participation is greatest at the top of Jonesville society and decreases on the way down the class hierarchy. The upper class belongs to the greatest number of associations, the upper-middle class next, and so on down to the lower-lower class which belongs to the least." Warner, *Democracy in Jonesville*, New York, 1949, p. 117. See also pp. 138, 140, 141, 143.

"A higher proportion of the members of the upper class belong to more associations than the members of any other class." Warner, *Jonesville*, p. 131.

"The upper and upper-middle classes are highly organized, well integrated social groups. The lower-middle and lower classes are more loosely organized and have fewer devices for maintaining their own distinctiveness in the community." Warner, *Jonesville*, p. 148. See also p. 153.

"Many organized groups touch only a few people in a community. Studies in cities reveal that 40 to 60 per cent of adults are members of these organized groups if church membership is excluded. In rural communities the percentage is smaller. So when we bring in representatives from these organized groups, we should not pretend that we are getting a complete representation of the people of the community. The American practice of 'joining' is not as universal as popularly assumed." G. W. Blackwell, "Community Analysis," *Approaches to the Study of Politics*, Roland Young, ed., Northwestern University Press, 1958, p. 306.

"Aside from church participation, most urban individuals belong to one organization or none. Low socio-economic rank individuals and middle-rank individuals, usually belong to one organization at most, and it is usually work-connected for men, child-church connected for women. Only in the upper socio-economic levels is the 'joiner' to be found with any frequency. When attendance at organizations is studied, some twenty per cent of the memberships are usually 'paper' memberships." Scott Greer, "Individual Participation in Mass Society," *Approaches to the Study of Politics*, p. 332.

25. Latham, *op. cit.*, pp. 35–36.

26. See *Reporter*, November 25, 1958, for story of Senator Bricker and the Ohio Right-to-Work referendum.

3

Whose Game
Do We Play?

THE scope and bias of the pressure system suggests some of
the limitations of pressure politics as a form of political organization. The limitations of pressure politics become more
evident when an attempt is made to use a pressure group in
some dimensions of politics other than the relatively narrow
range usually reserved for it.

Some of these limitations may be seen in our examination
of a number of pressure groups interested in general public
causes. What happens when pressure tactics are used to promote widely diffused interests? A survey of a few of these
might easily give rise to some skepticism about the effectiveness of pressure tactics in this area.

Are the public-spirited people who invest time, energy,
and money in these organizations playing the right game?
Would it not be intelligent to consider the relation between
the resources mobilized by these organizations and the proportions of the task undertaken by them? What scale of political organization is appropriate to the tasks assumed by
these groups?

What kind of "pressure" can the 350 members of the
Shore and Beach Preservation Association exert on Congress? Would it not be intelligent to recognize that this kind
of group is wholly dependent on the socialization of con-

Are the Political Resources of the Following Public-interest Pressure
Groups Adequate for the Tasks They Have Undertaken?

NAME OF ASSOCIATION	NUMBER OF MEMBERS
American League to Abolish Capital Punishment	720
National Child Labor Committee	15,000
American Civil Liberties Union	22,000
National Civil Service League	3,000
National Defense League of America	5,747
Foreign‑Policy Association	17,000
League for Industrial Democracy	3,000
National Municipal League	3,500
Navy League of the United States	10,000
National Planning Association	2,000
Public Education Association	2,000
American Public Welfare Association	5,000
National Safety Council	8,500
Shore and Beach Preservation Association	350
National Tax Association	2,100
National Tuberculosis Association	5,000
League of Women Voters of the United States	106,000
Common Council for American Unity	3,000
Planned Parenthood Federation of America	10,000
National Committee for Mental Hygiene	800
People's Lobby, Inc.	2,370

flict? This is a trigger organization which may start a chain
reaction, but what happens thereafter? Ultimately general
policies make demands on the political system as a whole.
Sooner or later we come to questions concerning the grand
strategy of American politics—for what shall it profit us if
we are organized to win all the little battles and lose all the
big ones? Is it enough to start a multitude of battles if we
cannot follow through?

In politics as in everything else it makes a great difference
whose game we play. The rules of the game determine the
requirements for success. Resources sufficient for success in

one game may be wholly inadequate in another. These considerations go to the heart of political strategy. The contrast between pressure politics and party politics becomes evident as soon as we try to transpose the players from one game to the other.

How small the pressure system is does not become clear until we attempt to convert pressure-group membership into party votes. A presidential election involves the greatest mobilization of political forces in the country; a good test of the significance of the pressure system in party politics is therefore to estimate the potential weight of special interests in a presidential election.

We can make a beginning by examining a number of public opinion polls taken during presidential campaigns to show the party preferences of some of the larger special-interest groups, groups of which organized labor is the largest. What is the impact of organized labor in these elections?

About 70 percent of *organized* labor (more pro-Democratic than nonunion labor) voted Democratic in 1940 and 1944 according to polls taken at the time. (The CIO membership voted 79 and 78 percent Democratic in these elections.) In a series of polls taken in 1936, 1943, 1944, 1945, and 1946, the Democratic party preference of organized labor was 72, 72, 64, 74, and 69 percent.[1] For the purposes of this calculation these figures may be taken as typical in spite of the fact that small variations in more recent elections have shown that organized labor may now be less strongly Democratic. That is to say, the statistics used here probably exaggerate the impact of organized labor slightly, as will be observed.

Some allowance must be made for the fact that it is never possible to convert the whole membership of any group into votes. The way in which the law of the imperfect political mobilization of social groups affects the calculus of politics is shown in the following model of the probable influence of the AFL-CIO in a typical election. The percentages and ratios shown are merely illustrative.

Organized Labor and Presidential Elections

Total membership of AFL-CIO	16,000,000
Since only about half of the membership votes in presidential elections, subtract	8,000,000
Votes actually cast by AFL-CIO members	8,000,000
Democratic share of the labor vote (70% of 8,000,000)	5,600,000
Republican share (30% of 8,000,000	2,400,000
Subtract Republican share of the labor vote from the Democratic share to get net Democratic gain	3,200,000

This analysis probably exaggerates the political weight of organized labor because it is doubtful that as many as half of labor union members actually vote in presidential elections. The 3,200,000 net contribution of organized labor to the Democratic total is important, but it is only one-fifth as great as it would have been if unions were able to control the vote of their whole membership.

The discussion has often been utterly confused by the tendency to attribute unanimity to special-interest groups. The law of the imperfect political mobilization of social groups forces us to revise the calculus of politics when we try to translate pressure-group power into party power.

The effect of *organization* is substantially less than the foregoing calculation suggests, however. For example, *a*

*substantial percentage of workers would have voted Demo-
cratic even if they had not belonged to unions.* A fairly typical set of polls shows the vote intentions of union members
and non-union workers in three presidential elections.

Union and Non-union Votes in Presidential Elections*

PER CENT DEMOCRATIC

YEAR	UNION MEMBERS	NONUNION MEMBERS
1944	72	56
1940	72	64
1936	80	72
Average	74.7	64

* *Gallup Political Almanac* (1946), p. 205.
See also Campbell and Cooper, *Group Differences in Attitudes and Votes,*
Survey Research Center, University of Michigan, 1956, pp. 54–55.

Apparently "organization" increases the Democratic bias
of workers about 10 percent. Now, if we apply this datum to
the 3,200,000 net Democratic gain, shown by the calculation on page 50, we get a new set of figures.

No mention is made here of the votes cast by the *wives* of
union members because nonunion workers and Republican
workers also have wives.

This calculation does not dispose of the matter because
there are some "iffy" elements in it, but it does raise a question about the voting power of organized labor. If AFL-CIO,
the largest special-interest group in the country, can swing
only about one million votes, what is the impact of ordinary
pressure groups likely to be? Pressure politics and party politics are two different things, and the impact of the one on
the other is not what it seems to be in a superficial analysis.

From the standpoint of party politics the margins within
which pressure groups operate are limited. *If a group di-*

Recalculation of Labor Vote in a Typical Presidential Election

Members AFL-CIO	16,000,000
Do not vote	8,000,000
	8,000,000
Do vote	8,000,000
64% who would probably have voted Democratic even if not organized by labor unions, subtract	5,120,000
36% who would probably have voted Republican if labor had not been organized, subtract	2,880,000
Net Democratic advantage (if workers had not been organized)	2,240,000
Net gain for Democrats as shown in previous calculation concerning the vote of organized labor	3,200,000
Net gain for Democrats if labor had not been organized, subtract	2,240,000
Net gain for Democratic party attributable to unionization	960,000

vides equally in an election, its impact is zero. On the other hand, it is unusual for much more than 70 percent of any large social group to support either of the parties. Thus for all practical purposes the "range" of discretion within which these groups operate is approximately 20 percent. Twenty percent of the membership is much less than the usual estimate of the impact of special-interest groups on party politics.

If we were to apply the calculation made in the case of organized labor to the American Bankers' Association (17,000 members), the end product would be insignificant, even if we make allowance for the probability that bankers are more highly mobilized than union members. As a matter of fact, nearly all business organizations are so small that the political mobilization of their members for voting purposes is pointless.

The impact of special-interest groups on party politics is further affected by the fact that they may actually have a *negative* effect in elections. Thus, in one poll, a cross section of American voters was asked how they would be influenced by the information that a candidate for Congress was endorsed by organized labor; the ratio of unfavorable to favorable responses was five to one.[2] If we follow the line of reasoning suggested by this poll, the calculus becomes something of a shambles.

The "reverse effect" of many special-interest organizations on party politics seems to be very strong. A 1944 poll indicated that the endorsement of candidates by the National Association of Manufacturers would have had marked adverse influence.[3]

A study made by the Washington Public Opinion Laboratory in 1950 showed that endorsements by each of thirteen well-known organizations was likely to have *some* adverse effect on the popularity of candidates.[4] All calculations of the influence of pressure groups in elections must take account of the *unpopularity of nearly all special-interest groups*. Pressure groups are not only small; they are widely disliked.

When allowance is made for all of the kinds of shrinkage (nonvoting, imperfect mobilization, tendency of divided votes to cancel out, and the reverse effect of special-interest groups), it becomes evident that *it is nearly impossible to translate pressure politics into party politics.* This discussion boils down to the proposition that pressure groups may have an impact on public opinion in general, but this is the point at which pressure politics ceases to be pressure politics.

Samuel Lubell refers to this factor when he writes (in formulating his new theory of party politics), "When any one element becomes disaffected, the power of antagonistic elements is automatically enhanced—and so is their attachment to the party. Precisely because the party elements are so hostile to one another, the bolt of one helps to unify the other."[5]

As a matter of fact, however, Lubell greatly exaggerates the group composition of the parties. The notion that parties are aggregates of special-interest groups held together by an endless process of negotiation and concession is unrealistic.

1. It underestimates the consequences of the fact that we have a two-party system. *The parties compete with each other;* they do not compete with pressure groups. The amount of bargaining that they have to do with special-interest groups is limited by the fact that each party must cope primarily with its *party* opposition. Neither party can afford to make excessive concessions to any pressure group.
2. A much better explanation of the process of majority formation is that majorities result automatically from the fact that we have a two-party system. In a two-party election one or the other of the parties is almost certain to get a majority. To win elections it is good strategy to appeal to the general public broadly on matters of general interest and above all to *keep an eye on the opposition party.*
3. The scope and bias of the pressure system do not fit easily into the calculus of party politics. First, *the pressure system is much too small to play the role sometimes assigned to it.* Secondly, the supposed party neutrality of the pressure groups is largely a myth.[6]

Since it is not easy to move special-interest groups from one party camp into the other, is it not better party strategy to try *to capitalize on the public hostility toward many of these groups than it is to woo them?* The shrinkage resulting from any attempt to convert pressure politics into party politics is so great that we might well conclude that it is never practical to attempt to translate one kind of political force into another.

It follows from the foregoing analysis that any description of political parties as aggregates of special-interest groups is not very convincing. Moreover, the notion that majorities can be formed by accumulating the support of a multitude of special-interest groups does not look like good political analysis because it substitutes a complex explanation for a simple one. If there are only two exits in a concert hall, it is extremely likely that more people will use one exit than the other. The two-party system produces majorities as simply as that![7]

Finally something ought to be said about the logical fallacy of the straw that broke the camel's back. The fable is that the camel was able to bear up under the weight of 999,999 straws but that his back was broken by the millionth straw. This venerable fallacy ignores the obvious truth that each of the million straws contributed equally to the breaking of the camel's back. Unfortunately this kind of logic has been perpetuated in the literature of pressure politics. In a concrete instance the argument runs as follows: Iowa corn growers, incensed at the Republican party for its failure to provide adequate storage facilities, switched from the Republican party to the Democratic party in 1948 and elected Mr. Truman President of the United States. Let us examine the reasoning behind this story.

It is true that Mr. Truman carried Iowa by 28,000 votes and that Iowa corn growers might conceivably have provided that many votes in the election. However, Mr. Truman polled 522,000 votes in Iowa in the 1948 election, and obviously each of these 522,000 votes contributed equally to his victory. A vote for Mr. Truman counted exactly as much in the final result whether it was cast by a corn grower or a plumber or a school teacher, since all votes are mathematically equal. This would have been true even if Mr. Truman had carried the state by a single vote. In that event every-

one who voted for Mr. Truman would have had an equal
claim to the honor of having cast the decisive vote.

The power of pressure groups tends to evaporate when it
is translated into other dimensions of politics because the
calculus of party politics is entirely different from the calculus of pressure politics. Numbers are everything in one dimension and very little in the other. We are dealing with
two different strategies of politics and two different concepts of political organization. Moreover, *the end product of
party politics is inevitably different from that of pressure
politics.* Inevitably some people prefer one game to the other.

Theoretically, pressure groups are nonpartisan (i.e., neutral in party conflict). The ancient assumption is that they
reward their friends and punish their enemies regardless of
party affiliation by throwing their weight either way as the
circumstances warrant.

Actually the neutrality of pressure groups in party politics
is largely a myth because political alignments are not as
fluid as this concept implies. It is at least as likely that pressure groups are prisoners of the parties as it is the other way
around, because pressure groups cannot easily negotiate
with both sides in the party conflict. If business groups can
do nothing but support the *Republican* candidates, *the Republican party dominates the pressure groups.* The Republican party enjoys a substantial latitude in its relations with
business because its only competitor is the Democratic party and business has no party alternative.[8]

The alignment in American politics does not array the
parties on the one side against a great mobilization of pressure groups on the other side. Rather, each of the major
parties attracts its own loose constellation of pressure
groups. Thus the contest aligns the Democratic party and its
ancillary groups against the Republican party and its affili-

ates. In this kind of alignment the relation of business and the Republican party is not that of master and servant (only the critics of the Republican party contend that it is the punching bag of business) because the party has what amounts to a political monopoly of the business interest. A party monopoly of any special interest implies that the *party* is the captor and the special-interest group is the captive.

The relation of business and the Republican party is much like that of organized labor and the Democratic party. Republican critics of the Democratic party like to portray the Democratic party as the slave of organized labor. Actually, labor usually has no place else to go. As long as it thinks that elections are important, it *must* support the Democratic party, generally. The facts of political life are that neither business nor labor is able to win elections by itself.

Once a two-party system is firmly established the major parties automatically have a monopoly of elections; they monopolize the greatest single channel to power in the whole regime. Control of elections gives the parties a very great position in the political system.

If there are twenty thousand pressure groups and two parties, who has the favorable bargaining position? In the face of this ratio it is unlikely that the pressure groups will be able to play off the parties against each other.

This analysis of the relations of pressure groups and political parties has been spelled out in some detail for a reason: *It has a bearing on the strategy of American politics.*

It has been necessary to show, first, that the parties are not the prisoners of the pressure groups. The second proposition follows from the first: The *public* has a choice of strategies. The public has a choice of strategies and theories of political organization as well as a choice of issues. As a matter of fact, the choice of issues is apt to be meaningless unless it is backed up by the kind of organization that can execute the mandate.

It is an axiom of warfare that military commanders try to force the fighting on the terrain best suited for the deployment of their own forces, but less well adapted for the deployment of the enemy forces. Thus a small army tries to force the enemy to fight on a battlefield so narrowly restricted that he cannot take advantage of his greater numbers, as the Spartans did at Thermopylae. It follows that there is a strategy for large numbers and a strategy for small numbers.

Pressure groups are small organizations that do not have the political resources to play in the great arena for the highest stakes. The big game is the party game because in the last analysis *there is no political substitute for victory in an election*. This is the doctrine of the chosen battlefield. A wise political leader chooses the arena in which he makes his bid for power.

The problem of party organization is so different from that of smaller associations that it is often misunderstood. Parties are usually compared with smaller organizations, nearly always to the disadvantage of the parties, but parties cannot be judged by the standards used to measure other organizations. The most obvious criterion of the adequacy of either of the major parties is its ability to cope with its party opposition. In other words the parties establish their own standards of adequacy. Most of the organizational problems of the parties are unique. The party system is by a wide margin the largest mobilization of people in the country. The parties lack many of the qualities of smaller organizations, but they have one overwhelming asset of their own. *They are the only organizations that can win elections.*

The parties solve their greatest organizational problem very simply by maintaining the two-party system. This system makes it possible for the parties to get along with structures far more rudimentary than would be necessary otherwise, because each has only to be able to compete with another equally vast and loosely organized opposition.

Anyone watching the crowds move about Grand Central Station might learn something about the nature of party organization. The crowds seem to be completely unorganized. What the spectator observes is not chaos, however, because the multitude is controlled by the timetables and the gates. Each member of the crowd finds his place in the system (is organized by the system) because his alternatives are limited.

The parties organize the electorate by reducing their alternatives to the extreme limit of simplification. This is the great act of organization. Since there are only two parties and both of them are very old, the veterans of a century of conflict, it is not difficult for people to find their places in the system. The rivalry is so old, it has been renewed so often, that the problem of identification and organization is very different from that of the new, little, transitory groups which are sometimes regarded as models of efficiency. Most Americans are veterans of the party wars; they know where they belong in the system.

Actually, the parties are the most competitive large organizations in American society. They are far more competitive than the churches, labor unions or business.

In the end, theories of power and political organization get themselves related to what people want to accomplish. Automatism and theories of the disintegration of politics grow out of the assumption that the community is so well established and so stable that no one needs to think about its future. On the other hand, concern for the survival of the community in tumultuous times calls for ideas about conscious control of events by the community and places a high value on the public interest, majority rule and political parties.

Assuming that the general interest in survival is strong enough to be organized we must assume also that this interest will seek its characteristic forms of political organization, organizations capable of exploiting the potentials of the political system. What is needed is a theory of political action able to serve this kind of demand.

Notes

1. Hadley Cantril, *Public Opinion, 1935–1946,* Princeton, 1951. 591, (2): 624 (9), 628 (18), 645 (7).

See also Campbell and Kahn, *The People Elect a President,* pp. 24 and 25, for data on the split of workers and farmers in the 1948 election.

2. American Institute of Public Opinion, September 7, 1938.

3. *Ibid.,* May 23, 1944.

4. See H. E. Freeman and Morris Showel, "Differential Political Influence of Voluntary Associations," *Public Opinion Quarterly* XV (1951), pp. 702 ff. The results of this study are less conclusive than they might have been if the authors had distinguished between organizations which are mutually exclusive and organizations which have no such directly antagonistic relations with rival organizations.

5. Samuel Lubell, *The Future of American Politics,* New York, 1952, p. 203.

6. "It isn't noticeable on the surface but a sweeping switchover is quietly taking place at the influence-peddling level in Washington. Democratic law firms are suddenly taking on GOP partners. New public-relations firms are springing up, and old ones are seeking influential Republican personnel." *Newsweek, "Periscope,"* December 8, 1952, p. 13.

7. Skepticism about the solidarity of two different religious groups has been expressed recently. See editorial by Elmo Roper, "the Myth of the Catholic Vote," *Saturday Review,* October 31, 1959, p. 22.

See also statement by Dr. Miriam K. Freund, president of Hadassah, quoted in the *New York Times,* February 1, 1960, as saying there is "no Jewish vote."

8. See letters to editor in *Wall Street Journal,* November 20, 1958.

4

The Displacement of Conflicts

WHAT happens in politics *depends on the way in which people are divided* into factions, parties, groups, classes, etc. The outcome of the game of politics depends on which of a multitude of possible conflicts gains the dominant position. The proposition may be illustrated by a simple diagram:

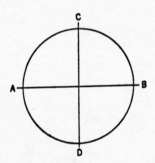

In this figure, the circle represents the political universe and the lines AB and CD are two possible lines of cleavage, among an infinite number of possibilities. The cleavages shown in the figure are completely inconsistent with each other; that is, a shift from one to the other involves a total reorganization of political alignments. Not only is the composition of each side changed as a result of the shift, but the conflict in the CD alignment is necessarily *about* something different from the conflict in the AB alignment, and the *outcome* of the conflict is therefore different. The political universe remains the same in spite of the shift, but what people can do and what they cannot do depends on how they are divided. Every shift of the line of cleavage affects the nature of the conflict, produces a new set of winners and losers and a new kind of result. Thus a change in the direction and location of the line of cleavage will determine the place of each individual in the political system, what side he is on, who else is on his side, who is opposed to him, how large the opposing sides are, what the conflict is about, and who wins. Since this is the process by which majorities and minorities are made, it may be said that every change in the direction and location of the line of cleavage produces a new majority and a new allocation of power.

The reader may want to amuse himself by playing with the idea outlined in the foregoing paragraph. Let us take an imaginary electorate and divide it in a number of different ways as follows:

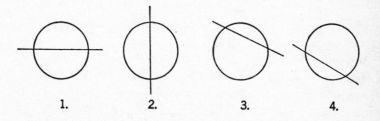

1. **2.** **3.** **4.**

It is obvious that the *meaning* of the contest and the allocation of power will be different in each of the four cases illustrated, even though the electorate remains the same. This is true because to a greater or lesser degree the antagonists change with every change in the cleavage.

The impact of any change in the lines of cleavage can be better understood if we take a closer look at what happens to the political universe when it is divided by a conflict. What are the preconditions for the development of a conflict? The evolution of a major conflict (important enough to call for a mobilization of opposing forces) involves an effort to consolidate people on both sides. Thus the conflict along the line XY in the figure below implies that an attempt is going to be made to unify the individuals in the area marked Aa against the individuals located in the area Bb. That is, a conflict presupposes the mobilization of people on both sides of the line of cleavage.

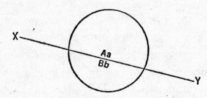

This is true because no conflict that amounts to more than a brawl can develop without a consolidation of the support of the opposing factions. It follows that conflicts divide people and unite them at the same time, and the process of consolidation is as integral to conflict as the process of division. The more fully the conflict is developed, the more intense it becomes, the more complete is the consolidation of the opposing camps. The failure to understand that *unification and division are a part of the same process* has produced some illusions about politics.

It follows from the foregoing analysis that political cleavages are extremely likely to be incompatible with each other. That is, the development of one conflict may inhibit the development of another because a radical shift of alignment becomes possible only at the cost of a change in the relations and priorities of all of the contestants.

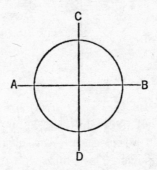

A shift from the alignment AB to the alignment CD means that the old cleavage must be played down if the new conflict is to be exploited. In this process friends become enemies and enemies become friends in a general reshuffle of relations. The new conflict can become dominant only if the old one is subordinated, or obscured, or forgotten, or loses its capacity to excite the contestants, or becomes irrelevant. Since it is impossible to keep the old and cultivate the new at the same time, *people must choose among conflicts.* In other words, conflicts compete with each other.

If the foregoing analysis is a good one, our concept of the nature of conflict must be reconsidered.

In the next figure, the real conflict may not be what it seems to be (a conflict between black and white along the line AB) but a conflict between the people who want to maintain the AB alignment and the relatively invisible people who want to start a new fight by shifting the cleavage from AB to CD of EF or GH. The motivations of people who

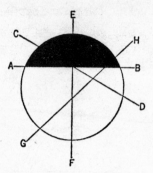

want to bring about these shifts of alignment are not difficult to understand because each new cleavage produces a
new allocation of power. The whites who are in power have
more reason for supporting the old alignment than the
blacks who are hopelessly out of power.

The calculus of politics becomes vastly more complex and
the potentialities are multiplied tremendously when we
move from the frontal attack of the whites on the blacks to
flank attacks designed to bring about a substitution of a new
conflict for the old one. The flank attack produces a conflict
of conflicts in which an attempt is made to displace the AB
alignment by another.

There are billions of potential conflicts in any modern society, but *only a few become significant.* The reduction of
the number of conflicts is an essential part of politics. Politics deals with the domination and subordination of conflicts. A democratic society is able to survive because it man-
ages conflict by establishing priorities among a multitude of
potential conflicts.

Any political system which attempted to exploit all of the
tensions in the community would be blown to bits. On the
other hand, every combination involves the dominance of

some conflicts and the subordination of others. Politics deals with the effort to *use* conflict. Every political party consists of discordant elements which are restrained by the fact that unity is the price of victory. The question always is: *Which battle do we want most to win?*

Since politics has its origin in strife, political strategy deals with the exploitation, use, and suppression of conflict. Conflict is so powerful an instrument of politics that all regimes are of necessity concerned with its management, with its use in governing, and with its effectiveness as an instrument of change, growth, and unity. The grand strategy of politics deals with public policy concerning conflict. This is the ultimate policy.

The most powerful instrument for the control of conflict is conflict itself. A generation ago E. A. Ross, a distinguished American sociologist, pointed out that conflicts tend to interfere with each other and that the very multiplicity of cleavages in a modern community tends to temper the severity of social antagonisms.[1]

The unstated assumption made by Professor Ross is that there is a kind of equality of conflicts. If this assumption were correct the rise of a multitude of inconsistent conflicts would tend to weaken all antagonisms in the community, producing a system of low-grade tensions. Is this assumption a reasonable one?

It is not much more reasonable to suppose that conflicts are of unequal intensity? Why should we assume that people are equally excited about all issues? On the other hand, what are the logical consequences of the inequality of conflicts? It seems reasonable to suppose that the more intense conflicts are likely to displace the less intense. What follows is a system of domination and subordination of conflicts. Therefore, every major conflict overwhelms, subordinates, and blots out a multitude of lesser ones.

The greatest hazard to any faction is not a frontal attack by the opposition but a flank attack by bigger, collateral, inconsistent, and irrelevant competitors for the attention and loyalty of the public. If there are degrees of intensity, the more intense will become dominant. The result is a reduction in the number of conflicts that can develop. The process is not to divide and divide and divide to infinity but to divide and unify as a part of the same process. For this reason it is probable that there exist a great number of potential conflicts in the community which cannot be developed because they are blotted out by stronger systems of antagonism. Thus the unequal intensity of conflicts determines the shape of the political system.

In the competition of conflicts there is nothing sacred about our preference for big or little conflicts. *All depends on what we want most.* The outcome is not determined merely by what people want but by their priorities. What they want more becomes the enemy of what they want less. Politics is therefore something like choosing a wife, rather than shopping in a five-and-ten-cent store.

The conflict of conflicts explains some things about politics that have long puzzled scholars. Political conflict is not like an intercollegiate debate in which the opponents agree in advance on a definition of the issues. As a matter of fact, *the definition of the alternatives is the supreme instrument of power;* the antagonists can rarely agree on what the issues are because power is involved in the definition. He who determines what politics is about runs the country, because the definition of the alternatives is the choice of conflicts, and the choice of conflicts allocates power. It follows that all conflict is confusing.

Historians describing armed conflict refer to this confusion as the "fog of war." A description of the battle of Gettysburg by Frank Aretas Haskell, a young officer attached to the staff of General Hancock, illustrates the point.

The wildest confusion for a few minutes obtained sway among us. The shells came bursting all about. The servants ran terror-stricken for dear life and disappeared. The horses, hitched to the trees or held by the slack hands of orderlies, neighed out in fright, and broke away and plunged riderless through the fields. The General at the first had snatched his sword, and started on foot for the front. I called for my horse; nobody responded. I had time to see one of the horses of our mess wagon struck and torn by a shell. The pair plunge—the driver has lost the reins—horses, driver and wagon go into a heap by a tree. Two mules close at hand, packed with boxes of ammunition, are knocked all to pieces by a shell. General Gibbon's groom has just mounted his horse and is starting to take the General's horse to him, when the flying iron meets him and tears open his breast. He drops dead and the horses gallop away. No more than a minute since the first shot was fired, and I am mounted and riding after the General. The mighty din now rises to heaven and shakes the earth. How the long streams of fire spout from the guns, how the rifled shells hiss, how the smoke deepens and rolls, but where is the infantry? Has it vanished in smoke? Is this a nightmare or a juggler's trick? . . . Who can describe such a conflict as is raging around us?[2]

If Haskell had been a political scientist he might have written a book to prove that Gettysburg was a sham battle because the lines were not neatly drawn.

The fog of political conflict is as impenetrable as the fog of war. Political conflicts are waged by coalitions of inferior interests held together by a dominant interest. The effort in all political struggle is to exploit cracks in the opposition while attempting to consolidate one's own side. Inevitably this results in many people saying many different things simultaneously.

One might match Haskell's account of the Battle of Gettysburg with Morton M. Hunt's account of the election of
1856, a truly fateful year in the history of American politics.

The political situation as it appeared after the conventions, was
supremely illogical. The Democrats approved of slavery and ap-
plauded the conduct of Representative Brooks and the Border Ruf-
fians, and at the same time they denounced the Republicans for
promoting religious intolerance and xenophobia. The Republicans,
liberal though they were, were working with the Northern Know-
Nothings. The regular Know-Nothing candidate, Fillmore, was
damned in the South as an Abolitionist and was damned in the
North for accepting as his running mate Andrew J. (Hundred-Nig-
ger) Donelson, a Southern planter who boasted of owning a hundred slaves. The Democrats charged the Republicans with being
Abolitionists, but William Lloyd Garrison angrily declared that the
Republican platform was a sellout to slavery, and his Abolitionist
Party ran its own hopeless campaign. The Irish and the Germans
were equally new to the country, and were equally detested by the
Know-Nothings, but all the former became Democrats and almost
all the latter became Republicans. Quite a few Know-Nothings in
New York, adhering to the Fillmore cause, managed to be simulta-
neously anti-Catholic, anti-foreigner, anti-Republican, anti-Border
Ruffian, and anti-Bully Brooks; if they were for anything, no one
knew what it was. And not only was the situation supremely illogical; it was supremely perilous for the country.[3]

All politics deals with the displacement of conflicts or efforts to resist the displacement of conflicts. The substitution
of conflicts looks like an argument about what the argument
is about, but politicians are not as confused as they seem to
be.[4]

If we must talk about politics in terms of conflict of interests, the least we might do is to stop talking about interests
as if they were free and equal. We need to discover the
hierarchies of unequal interests, of dominant and subordinate interests.

The crucial problem in politics is the management of conflict. No regime could endure which did not cope with this problem. All politics, all leadership, and all organization involves the management of conflict. All conflict allocates space in the political universe. The consequences of conflict are so important that it is inconceivable that any regime could survive without making an attempt to shape the system.

Americans hold more elections than all the rest of the world put together, but there must be millions of issues on which we cannot vote, or we cannot vote on them when we want to vote on them, or we cannot define them as we want to. A conclusive way of checking the rise of conflict is simply to provide no arena for it or to create no public agency with power to do anything about it. There are an incredible number of devices for checking the development of conflict within the system. Sectionalism is a device for submerging a whole order of conflicts. All legislative procedure is loaded with devices for controlling the flow of explosive materials into the governmental apparatus. All forms of political organization have a bias in favor of the exploitation of some kinds of conflict and the suppression of others because *organization is the mobilization of bias.* Some issues are organized into politics while others are organized out.

Perhaps it would not be an overstatement to say that there are Republican and Democratic concepts of political organization. The Democratic party tends to be proparty, while the Republican party tends to be antiparty. Much of the controversy about the future of the party system stems from the prevalence of partisan differences of opinion about purposes of political organization. This is not evidence of the meaninglessness of party politics but of its importance, for people do not invent competing theories of organization and strategy about unimportant things. In other words, the quarrel is as apt to be about the means as about the ends of politics.

The very fact that politics deals largely with procedure rather than substance (with power, institutions, concepts of organization, rights, and government, none of which is an end in itself) demonstrates its strategic character. We get confused about the meaning of politics because we underestimate the importance of strategy.

One difficulty scholars have experienced in interpreting American politics has always been that the grand strategy of politics has concerned itself first of all with the structure of institutions. The function of institutions is to channel conflict; institutions do not treat all forms of conflict impartially, just as football rules do not treat all forms of violence with indiscriminate equality.

Nobody knows what American politics would be like if we had the institutions to facilitate the development of a wider span of political competition. No matter what we do about the problem, however, it is unlikely that we shall ever become hospitable to all conflict, for the function of institutions is to discriminate among conflicts.

There is no more certain way to destroy the meaning of politics than to treat all issues as if they were free and equal. The inequality of issues simplifies the interpretation of politics. Politics becomes meaningful when we establish our priorities.

Since the displacement of conflicts is a prime instrument of political strategy, *what are the potentials of the strategy?* What are some of the raw materials of the strategy of displacement? An enumeration of some of the incompatible conflicts in modern politics may show how the substitution of issues works.

The use of racial antagonism by southern conservatives to keep poor whites in line or the use of a sharply sectional alignment to destroy the radical agrarian movement in the 1890s illustrates the uses to which the strategy can be put. The revival of sectional antagonism was used to drive a wedge between the western and southern branches of the Populist movement, to consolidate the sectional monopoly of the southern Bourbons. At the same time it enabled the right wing of the Republican party to make itself supreme in the North and West. More recently the nationalization of politics has been used to subordinate older sectional cleavages to a new nationwide division. Urban-rural conflict has been used to check the political success of the labor movment, McCarthyism has been used to destroy a variety of liberal causes, and the religious issue has been used to confuse a great variety of other causes. Classical instances are the conflict between international class war and nationalism, the Marxian attempt to subordinate all other conflict to class war, totalitarianism, the primacy of foreign policy, and the use of war to subordinate revolutionary movements. In the United States there has been a long history of attempts to substitute procedural conflict for substantive conflict and attempts to subordinate political conflict to nonpolitical, nonpartisan movements (i.e., to subordinate avowed conflicts to unavowed conflicts).[5]

In all of these instances the effect of the substitution of conflicts has been much the same as if some of the troops in a battle were to be wheeled about at right angles to their old positions to join some of their recent enemies in an attack on their former comrades in arms who had meanwhile joined forces with other segments of the enemy. Commanders who are not agile when this happens are likely to be left in possession of deserted battlefields. *The substitution of conflicts is the most devastating kind of political strategy.*

Alliances are formed and re-formed; fortresses, positions, alignments and combinations are destroyed or abandoned in a tremendous shuffle of forces redeployed to defend new positions or to take new strong points. In politics the most catastrophic force in the world is *the power of irrelevance which transmutes one conflict into another and turns all existing alignments inside out.*

In view of this analysis, the most obvious thing in the world is the fact that an issue does not become an issue merely because someone says it is. The stakes in making an issue are incalculably great. Millions of attempts are made, but an issue is produced only when the battle is joined.

Why do some movements succeed and others fail? Why do some ideas gain currency and acceptance while others do not? Why do some conflicts become dominant while others attract no support?[6]

Dominance is related to intensity and visibility, the capacity to blot out other issues. It is related also to the fact that some issues are able to relate themselves easily to clusters of parallel cleavages in the same general dimension. A successful alignment accumulates a tremendous body of hangerson. The question is: What other uses can be made of the power won by the dominant cleavage? Success depends also on the degree of dissatisfaction with the old alignment already in existence.

The number of the subordinated conflicts in any political system must always be great. Every cleavage works to the disadvantage of millions of people. All those whose claims have been subordinated have an interest in a new alignment. These are the restless elements. Hence the attempt to shift the direction of politics is never made in a vacuum.

Every defeated party, cause, or interest must decide whether or not it will continue to fight along the old lines or abandon the old fight and try to form a new combination.

The danger is that diehard minorities which want to continue the old fights *may simply freeze obsolete alignments* and become permanently isolated minorities.

The majority is held together by the alignment around which it was formed. It has a vested interest in the old lineup in which it confronts familiar antagonists already well identified in old contests. A new alignment is likely to confuse the majority; new alignments are usually designed to exploit tensions within the majority. Hence the fight is apt to be between the interests that benefit by the maintenance of the old alignments and those demanding a new deal. The very fact no alignment and those demanding a new deal. The very fact that no alignment can satisfy all interests equally makes the political system dynamic.

Tension is universal in any system of majority rule. This is as true of the majority as of the minority. The party in power is involved in hazardous choices usually not fully consistent with its original mandate. The task tends to become impossible as the party becomes overcommitted with the passage of time. Moreover, no party in power is ever able to do with perfect freedom what is politically most advantageous. To understand the nature of party conflict it is necessary to consider *the function of the cleavages exploited by the parties in their struggle for supremacy.* Since the development of cleavages is a prime instrument of power, the party which is able to make its definition of the issues prevail is likely to take over the government.

For this reason there is always a large number of unavowed conflicts. Some conflicts cannot be exploited because they are inconsistent with the dominant conflicts. Some controversies must be subordinated by both parties because neither side could survive the ensuing struggle. The conflict between the few and the many (the rich and the poor) is built into the American system, but no party could afford to espouse openly the cause of the few against the many. Democracy itself is the overriding issue in American politics, but it is impossible to take an openly antidemocratic position and survive. Neither of the major parties could afford to be pro- or anti-Catholic, prosegregation, or anti-immigrant, or come out for aboliton of the income tax or repeal of the social security system. There is a perpetual effort of the parties to isolate each other. To say it crudely, *all radical proposals for the reorganization of American politics propose to isolate the rich*. The parties cannot agree about these things because the schemes of one are the ruination of the other.

The parties may agree for reasons that are wholly inconsistent and contradictory. A conservative party may be willing to make concessions as the price of victory, whereas a liberal party may moderate its demands in order to widen its appeal. The parties may therefore arrive at the center by different routes, but each is apt to distrust the motives of the other.

It is not meant to suggest here that party leaders are conscienceless men lacking in conviction and wiling to take any position likely to get them into power. All that is intended is that power is utterly implicated in the conflict, and the problem of political leaders is made difficult by the fact that power, like money, is multifunctional. The priorities of political leaders are never easy to establish because every position taken is apt to have consequences for all other positions, especially when the stake is control of the most powerful government in the world.

Notes

1. See E. A. Ross, *Social Psychology*, Macmillan, 1909, Chapter XVII.
2. *Harvard Classics*, Charles W. Eliot, ed., Vol. 43, pp. 394–395.

3. "Annals of Politics: The Ordeal of John Charles Fremont," *New Yorker,* November 3, 1956.

4. See *New Republic,* April 6, 1959, p. 2, "On Monday, by a vote of 49 to 46, the Senate passed the $389 million distressed areas bill to give loans and grants where unemployment is chronic. It is similar to the bill Eisenhower vetoed last year and 700 percent more than he recommended.

"Undoubtedly Eisenhower will veto the bill, and the close vote shows he cannot be overriden. The point is the analysis of the score. The Democratics voted 45–16 for, the Republicans 4–30 against.

"Fourteen of the 16 Democrats who voted against the bill were Southerners. Mostly they are the haughty men who—with the the Republicans—control Congress by seniority committee chairmanships. There was Harry Byrd (Va.), chairman of the Finance Committee, Eastland (Miss.), chairman of Judiciary, McClellan (Ark.), chairman of Government Operations.

"They were affected by the last November's election hurricane: possibly they disapproved of it. They are the Norman nobles who govern England and continue to speak French. Their alliance with the 30 Republicans in this instance shows how strong is the traditional GOP-Dixie axis.

"But now look at the other side. Every one of the 17 newly-elected freshmen Democrats voted for the bill. They were the ones who gave it its bare, 3-vote majority. They average 15 or 20 years younger than the Dixiecrat seniors. If they can stamp their party with liberalism the future belongs to them. Already they can occasionally tip the balance. In fairness to Lyndon Johnson, he voted with them on this occasion."

This is a conflict among factions having *opposing interests in the maintenance of an old alignment.*

5. Irwin Ross, describing the work of Whitaker and Baxter, a public relations firm active in California politics, says of one of their campaigns, "Their strategy was the ultimate in what might be called the divisionary technique," *Harpers Magazine,* vol. 219, no. 1310, July, 1959, p. 56.

6. See Lillian Smith, article in *New Republic,* December, 1957, for a theory of action and control.

5

The Nationalization
of Politics

A CASE STUDY IN THE CHANGING
DIMENSIONS OF POLITICS[1]

To understand what has happened in American politics in
the past generation it is necessary to go back to the election
of 1896, one of the decisive elections in American history. It
is necessary to understand what happened in 1896 in order
to understand the Republican party system, which dominated the country in the first third of this century.

How was it possible for the conservative wing of the Republican party to gain the great ascendancy in American
politics which it enjoyed during the first generation of the
twentieth century? The 1896 party alignment is important
to an understanding of the situation (1) because it was remarkably stable and (2) because it was powerful enough to
determine the nature of American politics for more than
thirty years. The 1896 party cleavage resulted from the tremendous reaction of conservatives in both major parties to
the Populist movement, a radical agrarian agitation that
alarmed people of substance all over the country. The
movement spread over wide areas west of the Mississippi in
the late 1880s, then swept into the South, where in 1890 it

captured control of no less than eight state legislatures. Southern conservatives reacted so strongly that they were willing to revive the tensions and animosities of the Civil War and the Reconstruction in order to set up a one-party sectional southern political monopoly in which nearly all Negroes and many poor whites were disfranchised. One of the most important consequences of the creation of the Solid South was that it severed permanently the connection between the western and the southern wings of the Populist movement.

The second stage of the conservative reaction to Populism occurred in 1896, when William Jennings Bryan and his supporters took control of the Democratic National Convention, negotiated a Democratic-Populist fusion, and nominated Bryan for the Presidency on a Populist platform.

The northern conservatives were so badly frightened by the Bryan candidacy that they adopted drastic measures to alarm the country. As a matter of fact, the conservative reaction to Bryanism in the North was almost as spectacular as the conservative reaction to Populism in the South. As a result the Democratic party in large areas of the Northeast and Middle West was wiped out, or decimated, while the Republican party consolidated its supremacy in all of the most populous areas of the country. The resulting party lineup was one of the most sharply sectional political divisions in American history. In effect, the new party division turned the country over to two powerful sectional minorities: (1) the northern business-Republican minority and (2) its southern conservative Democratic counterpart.

The new alignment became possible when the southern conservative Democrats decided that they were willing to abandon their ambitions to win power nationally in return for undisputed control of the South. The Solid South was one of the foundation stones of the Republican system because it weakened the Democratic party disastrously and virtually destroyed for a generation the possibility of an effective national opposition party.

From the standpoint of national politics the principal function of the Solid South was to make impossible a combination of the southern and western agrarian radicals. On the other hand, the establishment of a one-party system in the South simplified tremendously the task of the Republican conservatives because *it isolated the western radical wing of the party.* Thereafter, the western Republican insurgents had no place to go; unable to make any combination able to win a national election, they were reduced to launching a succession of futile sectional minor parties.

The ascendancy of the conservative wing of the Republican party was made possible, in the second place, by the extreme sectionalism of the alignment. Sectionalism in the North was only superficially less intense than in the South. In large areas of both sections the opposition party was extinguished or became ineffective. The result was that organized party alternatives disappeared in large areas of the country in the North as well as the South. Both sections became more conservative because *one-party politics tends strongly to vest political power in the hands of people who already have economic power.* Moreover, in one-party areas (areas of extreme sectionalism) votes decline in value because the voters no longer have a valuable party alternative.

What emerges from a study of the crisis of 1896 is the realization that the newly successful combination was able *to make use of two contradictory and inconsistent conflicts to capture power.* The Bryan-Democratic-Populist attack on the conservatives in both parties cut across the old sectional cleavage based on antagonisms of the Civil War and the Reconstruction. The result was a conflict of conflicts in

The 1896 System

*(Based on the antagonistic collaboration of two
conservative sectional minorities)*

Solid South (Democratic): Represented a willingness to abandon presidential politics in return
for undisputed supremacy in the southern states
and a free hand to treat the race issue as a local
southern problem.

Almost Equally Solid North (Republican): Designed to give big business a free hand to exploit their dominant position in the economy,
based on the presidential veto, judicial review,
the appointing power (refusal to enforce laws),
and obstructive legislative tactics.

which the antagonists in one contest joined hands and ex-
changed partners in the other.

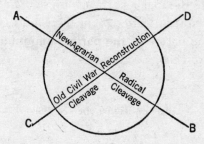

The contradiction between the old and the new conflicts
furnished the raw material for reorganization of American
politics along the lines of the 1896 cleavage.

Thus, the southern Democratic conservatives and the
northern Republican conservatives joyfully revived the old
sectional conflict in order to split the Populist movement.
The establishment of the alignment of 1896 is perhaps the
best example in American history of the successful substitu-

tion of one conflict for another. The radicals were defeated because the conflict they sought to exploit was subordinated to an inconsistent cleavage which split the radical movement, isolated the southern and western radicals from each other, and overwhelmed both wings in one-party sectional alignments. On the other hand, the conservatives won power because they were able to impose on the country the conflict which divided the people the way they wanted them to be divided. The very nature of the new alignment made open collaboration between the northern conservative Republicans and the southern conservative Democrats impossible, but the *de facto*, under-the-table alliance was the foundation stone of the Republican system.

A study of election returns will show what the new alignment looked like.

Before 1896 the major parties contested elections on remarkably equal terms throughout the country. Election returns show the nature of the party equilibrium in the two decades before 1896.

Election Returns before 1896

YEAR	REPUBLICAN	DEMOCRATIC
1876	4,036,296	4,300,590
1880	4,454,416	4,444,952
1884	4,854,891	4,914,986
1888	5,439,853	5,540,329

Even in 1892, in spite of the Populist candidacy of General Weaver, the difference between the Democratic and Republican presidential vote was only 380,000 in a national total of about 12,000,000.

The effect of the election of 1896 is shown by a comparison of the party vote in 1892 and 1896 in a number of states outside the Solid South (see table below).

Sample Comparison of Election Returns, 1892 and 1896

STATE		1892		1896
Connecticut	D	82,395	D	56,740
	R	77,025	R	110,285
Illinois	D	426,281	D	464,523
	R	399,288	R	607,148
New Hampshire	D	42,081	D	21,271
	R	45,658	R	57,444
New Jersey	D	177,042	D	133,675
	R	156,068	R	221,367
New York	D	654,868	D	551,369
	R	609,350	R	819,838
Pennsylvania	D	452,264	D	427,125
	R	516,011	R	728,300
Rhode Island	D	24,335	D	14,459
	R	26,972	R	37,437
Wisconsin	D	177,335	D	165,523
	R	170,791	R	268,135

In 1892 there were thirty-six states in which on the face of the returns something like a competitive party situation existed. By 1904 there remained only six states in which the parties were evenly matched, while there were thirty states in which the situation could no longer be described as competitive.

The decline of party competition was greatest in the South. In 1884, before the Populist invasion, the Republican

Republican Vote in Certain Southern States in 1884 and 1904

STATE	1884	1904
South Carolina	21,733	2,570
Florida	28,031	8,314
Alabama	59,591	22,472
Mississippi	43,509	3,280
Louisiana	46,347	5,205

vote was less than half of the Democratic vote in only three southern states—South Carolina, Texas, and Georgia.

A comparison of the Republican vote in 1884 and 1904 shows what the new lineup did to southern politics. However, the alignment after 1896 not only curtailed party competition, it reduced over-all participation in elections. The decline of the total vote cast in the South is shown by comparison of the vote in 1884 and 1904 given below.

Total Vote Cast in South

STATE	1884	1904
Louisiana	108,887	54,947
Mississippi	120,019	58,721
South Carolina	91,623	55,670
Texas	318,450	233,919
Virginia	324,853	130,842

The new sectionalism had a similar effect throughout the country. In fourteen states outside the South the total vote was less in 1904 than in 1896. It is profoundly symptomatic of the new condition of politics that the election of 1904 produced the first popular presidential election landslide in American history and did so in a declining total vote.

The results of the big Republican monopoly in the North and the little Democratic monopoly in the South were much the same. The strength of the Republican party in the thirty-one states outside of the South and the border states is shown by the fact that the Democratic party carried only about an average of two of these states in each presidential election between 1896 and 1932.

Party competition survived in the border states and was sometimes important in New York, Ohio, and Indiana, but the contests elsewhere in the United States were nearly always so one-sided that the voters had no significant choices. The extension of one-party areas meant that in 1904 less than one seventh of the population of the United States lived in states in which the parties contested the election on relatively equal terms, while in 1920 only about 12 million out of 105 million Americans lived in states in which they had a choice between two major parties both of which had a chance to win.

Sectionalism tends strongly to depress party organization because elections in one-party areas are won not by competing with the opposition party but by eliminating it. After 1896 there were large areas of the North in which the Democratic party virtually ceased to exist. In large areas of the North, Democratic representation in state legislatures became nearly extinct. In other places, weak local Democratic organizations were absorbed by powerful Republican machines in bipartisan local systems.

All that might be said about the decadence of the Democratic party in the North was twice as true of the Republican party in the South. The dominant party organizations, North and South, became the administrators of regional political monopolies.

The Revolution of 1932

In 1932 the country, in the midst of a great depression, used a demoralized and disorganized Democratic party to produce the greatest reversal of public policy in American history. This happened not because the Democratic party was an ideal vehicle for this task but because it was the only instrument available. The election of 1932 was much more than the defeat of a political party; it was something very much like the overthrow of a ruling class. The Democratic party in the 1930s became the reluctant instrument of a revolution it did not plan and did not produce. It is hard to imagine a party less prepared for its new responsibilities than the Democratic party was at the time of Franklin Roosevelt's first inaugural. The fact that the country used the Democratic party to produce the first party turnover in more than a generation contributed greatly to the development of a new concept of the function of the party system, a renewed interest in the idea of party responsibility.

A comparison of the policy of the Democratic party before and after the election of Franklin Roosevelt will show the difference between the old and the new functions of the party system.

A look at the Democratic platform of 1912 on the eve of the election of Woodrow Wilson is sufficient to show the party's thinking. In 1912 Democrats talked about the preservation of the rights of the states and condemned as "usurpation" the efforts of the Republican party "to enlarge and magnify by indirection the powers of the Federal government." They argued that the protective tariff was unconstitutional. The general attitude of the party toward the function and scope of the national government is shown in their criticism of "the profligate waste of money wrung from the people by oppressive taxation through lavish appropriations which have kept taxes high and reduced the purchasing power of the people's toil." (Expenditures by the federal government in 1912 were about two thirds of a billion dollars.)

Otherwise the party declared its support of the system of separation of powers and came out for the direct election of senators, for a presidential primary, and for a constitutional amendment limiting the President to one term. In other major areas of public policy the program may be summarized as follows:

1. Labor—The Democratic party wanted to restrict the use of injunctions, favored the creation of a Department of Labor, and advocated a federal employees' compensation set "as far as the federal jurisdiction extends."

2. Agriculture—It sought an extension of rural credits, expansion of rural free delivery of mail, and opposed gambling in agricultural commodities.

3. Business—The party wanted to reduce tariffs, tighten antitrust laws, and strengthen the regulation of railroad rates, favored development of waterways and conservation of natural resources, and opposed the creation of a central bank dominated by the "money trust."

4. Social Services—Democrats wanted a parcel post system and favored establishment of a single national health agency, but socialized medicine was unheard of.

5. Foreign Policy—The Democratic party supported the Monroe Doctrine and urged a cautious expansion of the Navy.

Finally, the party supported the income tax amendment to the Constitution, but it is highly improbable that it foresaw the scale on which this new form of taxation is used today.

This summary is not made to show that the Democratic party has been inconsistent but to illustrate the thesis that *the party realignment of 1932 is closely related to a profound change in the agenda of American politics.* An examination of both platforms of 1912 shows how little difference there was between the Republican and Democratic parties at that time.

An analysis of the operations of American government before World War I shows that the party platforms of 1912 did not depart greatly from the actual condition of public affairs at that time. In 1915 the government spent 760 million dollars, of which about one third went to the armed forces and an almost equal amount to support the civil functions of the government, while another third was spent on veterans, refunds, interest, and debt retirement. The government had not yet got around to adopting a budget system.

About two thousand persons were sent to federal prisons in 1915 convicted of offenses such as counterfeiting and forgery, drug act violations, immigration-act offenses, or violation of the interstate commerce act, liquor laws, the Mann Act, and the postal laws. The new income tax hardly scratched the surface of the economy; 337,000 persons made returns and paid a total of forty-one million dollars.

Apart from the postal service and the management of the currency, the federal government touched directly only a few categories of people: its own employees, importers, interstate processors and dealers in certain foods and drugs, physicians and druggists who handled narcotics, the liquor business, the managers of interstate railroads, Indians, people engaged in navigation, people who collected excise taxes, certain contractors, immigrants, corporation lawyers and financiers, counterfeiters, and white slavers.

It is hardly necessary to document the proposition that the change in public policy that followed the 1932 election was the greatest in American history. However, the New Deal itself was in its turn swamped a decade later by an even greater revolution in foreign policy arising from World War II and the Cold War. The cumulative effect of two revolutions has been to produce what is virtually a new government and a new political base for American public policy.

Thus a change in the party alignment, the way the two parties divided the nation, was accompanied by a great change in the meaning of American politics and the nature of the party alternatives. The election of 1932 produced the largest displacement of conflicts in American history and greatly enlarged the scope of party competition. The involvement of the American public in American politics underwent a profound transformation as a result of the substitution of the 1932 alignment for the 1896 alignment.

What happened to the party alignment after 1932? The elections since 1932 have *substituted a national political alignment for an extreme sectional alignment everywhere in the country except the South.* Graphically, the nationalization of American politics can be seen in *the flattening of the curve showing the percentage distribution of the major party vote outside the South.*

The flattening of the curve can be expressed statistically by the percentage of the major party vote polled by the Democratic party in each of the states, taking into account the deviation from 50 percent in each case. (Thus 44 and 55 percent represent deviations of 6 and 5 percent, respectively.) In the election of 1908 in twenty-nine states in the North and West (not counting Arizona and New Mexico), the Democratic percentage of the major party vote deviated a total of 283.8 points from 50 percent. In 1928 the total deviation was 312.1. By 1944, however, this figure had declined to 124 points. In other words, the 1944 curve was almost three times as flat as the 1928 curve. This is only another way of saying that there has been a sharp decline in the number of one-party states. In 1944, outside the South and the border states, the Democratic party polled more than 60 percent or less than 40 percent of the major party vote in only two states, and a shift of 3 percent of the major party vote would have changed the result in seventeen states.

The figures show that elections are now dominated by factors that work on a national scale. One result has been *a very great extension of the area of party competition.*

What did the elections of 1952 and 1956 do to the new party alignments? They did nothing to reverse the nationalizing tendency of American politics and gave no indication whatever of a tendency to return to the old sectional pattern of politics, in spite of the party turnover.

These elections were as completely dominated by national influences as were the Democratic elections of 1932, 1936, 1940, 1944, and 1948. *The direction and the scope of the cleavage between the major parties have remained stable in spite of the fact that it was the Republican party that now profited by the new dimension of politics. We are, for the first time in American history, within striking distance of a competitive two-party system throughout the country,* and the nationalizing tendency has continued regardless of which of the parties is successful.

The position of the Solid South in American politics was altered beyond recognition by the fact that in four successive elections Mr. Roosevelt proved that he did not need the support of the southern wing of the party to be elected; in each of these elections he would have won with one hundred electoral votes to spare if he had received no votes at all south of the Mason-Dixon line.

The impact of the nationalization of politics on the Republican party is illustrated by the fact that the Eisenhower-Taft contest for the presidential nomination in 1952 produced some kind of split in thirty-eight of the state delegations at the Republican National Convention.

What is likely to be the effect of the nationalization of politics on *the frequency with which the parties alternate in power?* The question is important because the parties cannot be held responsible to the public if one party is in power permanently. The development of a competitive two-party system in all parts of the United States increases the importance of the opposition tremendously. So long as the party alignment was sharply sectional, the opposition could do little more than intensify the sectional cleavage; the more sharply the sectional alignment was drawn, the more deeply the party in power was intrenched. Sectionalism produced alignments which could rarely be overthrown by merely sectional attacks. Every sectional assault on the Republican party before 1932 served merely to increase the Republican margin in the great populous regions in which it was supreme, while it tended at the same time to intensify Democratic supremacy in the South. In a political system in which one great bloc of states confronts another bloc of states no ordinary shift of opinion is likely to have any important political effect; a general shift of the vote has little effect, because the margin of superiority of each of the parties in its own sectional base is so great that no ordinary movement of voters can overturn the alignment. This is not true in a national party alignment, where a shift of a few percent of the voters is likely to produce the greatest possible consequences. *One of the most significant consequences of the nationalization of politics in the last twenty years, therefore, has been the increased likelihood of a relatively frequent alternation of the parties in power.*

*fore, has been the increased likelihood of a relatively fre-
quent alternation of the parties in power.*

Democratic Vote in Certain Northern and Western States
in 1924 and 1952

STATE	1924	1952
Connecticut	110,184	481,649
Pennsylvania	409,192	2,146,269
Michigan	152,359	1,230,657
Illinois	576,975	2,013,920
Wisconsin	68,115	622,175
Minnesota	55,913	608,458
California	105,514	2,197,548
Ohio	477,887	1,600,367
Massachusetts	280,831	1,083,525
New Jersey	279,743	1,015,092
North Dakota	13,858	76,694
Washington	42,842	492,845
Total	2,573,413	13,569,199

The consequences of an increase in the rate of party alternation in power may be important. The party in power is
now forced to realize that it really can be turned out at the
next election. It is difficult to exaggerate the probable impact of this development on the programs, the organizations, the responsibilities, and the reputation and importance of the major parties.

The nationalization of politics, by increasing the likelihood of relatively frequent alterations of the parties in power, greatly *enhances the importance of elections and of elec-
tioneering political organizations.* It is noteworthy that the
presidential vote rose from twenty-nine million to more
than sixty-two million between 1924 and 1956. This increase is closely related to the extension of the area of competition in a national party alignment.

*The universality of political trends is an index of the na-
tionalization of the political system.* Does the same trend

Republican Vote in Eleven Southern States in 1924 and 1952

STATE	1924	1952
Virginia	73,328	306,925
North Carolina	190,754	558,107
South Carolina	1,123	168,082
Georgia	30,300	198,979
Florida	30,633	544,036
Tennessee	130,831	446,147
Alabama	42,823	149,231
Mississippi	8,494	112,966
Arkansas	40,583	177,155
Louisana	24,670	306,925
Texas	130,194	1,102,878
Total	703,733	4,071,431

appear throughout the country, or do conflicting trends appear? In a sectional political alignment one might expect to find Democratic and Republican trends appearing simultaneously in various parts of the country. Thus, in 1904 the Republican party won by a popular landslide, but the Republican party gained ground in only twenty-six states, while it lost ground in nineteen. In other words, the election produced two opposing trends.

We ought to suspect that something has happened to the political system when we observe that the Republican party gained ground in *every* state in 1952 and lost ground in forty-five states in 1954, gained ground throughout the country in 1956 and lost ground in nearly every state in 1958. These trends are national in scope. Moreover the nationalization of politics does not seem to have been affected by the fact that there has been a double party turnover in these elections.

What is the impact of the nationalization of politics on party organization likely to be? The reorganization of the

American party system is largely a matter of developing
new competing organizations in states that, until recently,
were dominated by a one-party system. This process goes on
at different rates throughout the country and at various levels of government. Commentators have noted that Republican gains in the South in the 1952 election did not produce
a reorganization of politics at the local level, but party reorganization throughout the old one-party states in the North
and West since 1932 has regularly developed first in presidential elections. Symptomatic of the new condition of
American politics is the fact that the Republican party made
a major organizing effort in the southern states in 1952 and
1956.

It is obvious that a national political system calls for a very
different kind of organization from that required in a sectional alignment. More precisely, a national alignment creates a demand for political organization throughout the
country, whereas sectionalism depresses national organizations. What has happened since 1932, therefore, has been a
great extension of organization into the newly developed
two-party regions.

One consequence of the nationalization of American politics is the reversal of the historic political policy of the Solid
South in the presidential candidacy of Lyndon Johnson in
1960. Senator Johnson's serious candidacy is obviously an
attempt to explore the new potentials of a nationalized system of politics. It reverses the abandonment of the presidential ambitions of southern political leaders implicit in the
creation of the Solid South and proves that when the southern system breaks up we shall not lack for southern leadership able and willing to take advantage of the situation. On
the other hand, is it not true that nearly everything that has
been said about the unsatisfactory condition of American
parties has been due to the existence of the old Solid South?

One of the discoveries made in a recent survey of politics[2] is that "very few of the state delegations to the national conventions in 1952 were within the grip of a recognized political boss." This conclusion is important because it is based on the first comprehensive national survey of American politics ever made. Evidence of the decline of the local party boss suggests that a profound change in the character of the party system has already taken place. It involves a shift in the locus of power within the party system; indeed, it involves a changed concept of power itself. Considering the role played by the local boss in the literature of American politics it now seems likely that the whole body of traditional propositions descriptive of the political system must be revised.

The major parties are now the most highly competitive large-scale organizations in American society, more competitive than business (which usually competes marginally) or the churches or the labor unions. The area and scale of party competition have been expanded greatly by the extension of the two-party system and by the establishment of the conditions for a much more rapid alternation of the parties in power. Competition on this scale provides powerful incentive for organization. It tends strongly to draw all political organizations, i.e., the pressure groups, Congress, etc., into the vortex of party conflict.

In terms of the political concepts outlined in this volume the change from sectional party cleavages to a national alignment is certain to enlarge the scope of conflict and to result in the rise and dominance of an entirely new order of conflicts.

One consequence of the development of the national dimension of politics is likely to be the creation of a national electorate and a national majority. The Presidency as the political instrument of this new constituency is likely to become more powerful.

Elections are now won and lost in the great urban-industrial belt extending from the northern Atlantic coast to the Pacific. On the other hand, the only way that the southern states can get back into presidential politics is to abandon their one-party sectional system; no amount of congressional politics is ever likely to compensate the South for its exclusion from the Presidency.

Notes

1. Some of the materials in this chapter first appeared in the chapter, "United States: The Functional Approach to Party Government," in Sigmund Neumann, *Modern Political Parties,* Chicago, 1956, pp. 194 ff. Reproduced here with permission of The University of Chicago Press.

2. Paul T. David, Malcolm Moos, and Ralph M. Goldman (eds.), *Presidential Nominating Politics, 1952,* John Hopkins Press, Baltimore, 1954.

If forty million adult citizens were disfranchised by law, we would consider that fact the first datum about the system. It may be even more important that this result has been accomplished by extra legal means.

Obviously, no political system could achieve 100 percent participation in elections. Even when full allowance is made, however, the scale of nonvoting in the United States is so great that it calls for some explanation beyond the various psychological and educational factors usually cited.[1]

The blackout of the forty million or so calls for a re-examination of the whole system. Nonvoting on this scale sheds a strange light on American democracy because it points up a profound contradiction between theory and practice. In this chapter, we shall discuss the nonvoting millions as a study in the scope, intensity, and bias of the political system.

With some important exceptions, the most striking fact about the phenomenon is that it seems to be voluntary. Outside the South, it has not been considered necessary to erect barriers against an invasion of the political system by the nonvoters, and no one seems about to do so. The community is willing to live with the hazards of a stiuation that places a curtain—a tissue-paper curtain, but still a curtain—between the participants and the nonparticipants. If the abstention of several tens of millions makes a difference, as it almost certainly does, we are forced to conclude that we are governed by invisible forces, for to an astonishing extent the sixty million are at the mercy of the rest of the nation which could swamp all existing political alignments if it chose to do so. The whole balance of power in the political system could be overturned by a massive invasion of the political system, and nothing tangible protects the system against the flood. All that is necessary to produce the most painless revolution in history, the first revolution ever legalized and legitimatized in advance, is to have a sufficient number of people do something not much more difficult than to walk across the street on election day.

Every regime lives on a body of dogma, self-justification, glorification, and propaganda about itself. In the United States, this body of dogma and tradition centers about democracy. The hero of the system is the voter who is commonly described as the ultimate source of all authority. The fact that something like forty million adult Americans are so unresponsive to the regime that they do not trouble to vote is the single most truly remarkable fact about it. In the past seven presidential elections, the average difference in the vote cast for the winning and the losing candidates was about one fifth as large as the total number of nonvoters. The unused political potential is sufficient to blow the United States off the face of the earth.

Why should anyone worry about twenty or thirty or forty million American adults who seem to be willing to remain on the outside looking in? What difference do they make? Several things may be said. First, anything that looks like a rejection of the political system by so large a fraction of the population is a matter of great importance. Second, anything that looks like a limitation of the expanding universe of politics is certain to have great practical consequences. Does nonvoting shed light on the bias and the limitations of the political system?

In American history, every change in the scope of the political system has had an impact on the meaning and operation of the system. Broadly speaking, the expansion of the political community has been one of the principal means of producing change in public policy; expansion has been the grand strategy of American politics. Every major change in public policy (the Jefferson, Jackson, Lincoln, and Roosevelt revolutions) has been associated with an enlargement of the electorate. Has something gone wrong with the

basic pattern of American politics? Has the political system
run out of gas? Have we lost the capacity to use the growth
of the electorate to provide a new base for public policy? If
we have lost the capacity to involve an expanding public in
the political system, it is obvious that American democracy
has arrived at a turning point.

What kind of system is this in which only a little more
than half of us participate? Is the system actually what we
have been brought up to think it is?

One of the easiest victories of the democratic cause in
American history has been the struggle for the extension of
the suffrage. After a few skirmishes in the first decades of
the nineteenth century, the barriers against male suffrage
gave way all along the line. A generation ago one distinguished United States senator was in the habit of saying that
rivers of blood have been shed for the right to vote. No
greater inversion of the truth is conceivable. The struggle
for the ballot was almost bloodless, almost completely
peaceful, and astonishingly easy. Indeed the bulk of the
newly enfranchised, including Negroes and nearly all wom-
en, won battles they never fought. The whole thing has
been deceptively easy. Somewhere along the line the antidemocratic forces simply abandoned the field. It is hard for
Americans to believe how easy it was because they have a
hopelessly romantic view of the history of democracy which
attributes a revolutionary significance to the extension of
the legal right to vote.

The expansion of the electorate was largely a by-product
of the system of party conflict. The rise of the party system
led to a competitive expansion of the market for politics.
The newly enfranchised had about as much to do with the
extension of the suffrage as the consuming public has had to
do with the expanding market for toothpaste. The parties,
assisted by some excited minorities, were the entrepre-

neurs, took the initiative, and got the law of the franchise liberalized. It has always been true that one of the best ways to win a fight is to widen the scope of the conflict, and the effort to widen the involvement of the more or less innocent bystanders produced universal suffrage. Our understanding of this development has been greatly confused by the compulsion to interpret our past in terms of the classical definition of democracy, which inevitably assigns a dramatic place in history to the seizure of power by the people.

The meaning of political competition in the expansion of the electorate is illuminated by the experience of the Solid South. The South is the last remaining area in the United States in which the struggle against democracy is carried on in terms of legal and extralegal restrictions of the right to vote. The southern states were able to exclude the Negro from the political system only by establishing a political monopoly. Once established the system has been used not only to disfranchise Negroes but also to depress political participation generally.

The socialization of politics as far as the right to vote is concerned has now been nearly complete for a generation, but the *use* of the ballot as an effective instrument of democratic politics is something else altogether. This is the point at which the breach between theory and practice of American democracy appears to be widest. If we do not understand what this breach is about, we simply do not understand American politics. The question is: If the conflict system is responsible for the extension of the legal right to vote, is it also responsible for limiting the practice of voting?

It is reasonable to look for some of the causes of massive self-disfranchisement in the operation of the political system. What is there about the system that depresses participation? Obviously, the relation of the electorate to the government is not so simple as it is commonly supposed to be.

The American political system is less able to use the democratic device of majority rule than almost any other modern democracy. Nearly everyone makes obeisance to the majority, but the idea of majority rule has not been well institutionalized and has never been fully legitimatized. The explanation of the ambivalence of the system is historical.

Democracy as we now understand it has been superimposed on an old governmental structure which was inhospitable to the idea. The result is a remarkable makeshift. Resistance to the growth of the political community has taken the form of attacks on all efforts to organize the majority, attacks on politics, politicians, and political parties. The offspring of this mixed parentage is a kind of monstrosity, a nonpolitical antimajoritarian democracy.

Massive nonvoting in the United States makes sense if we think of American government as a political system in which the struggle for democracy is still going on. The struggle is no longer about the *right to vote* but about the *organization of politics*. Nowadays the fight for democracy takes the form of a struggle over theories of organization, over the right to organize and the rights of political organizations, i.e., about the kinds of things that make the vote valuable.

Another way of saying the same thing is to say that the vote can be vitiated as effectively by placing obstacles in the way of organizing the electorate as if there were a denial of the right to vote. Nonvoting is related to the contradiction, imbedded in the political system, between (1) the movement to universalize suffrage and (2) the attempt to make the vote meaningless. We get confused because we assume that the fight for democracy was won a long time ago. We would find it easier to understand what is going on if we assumed that the battle for democracy is still going on but has now assumed a new form.

The success or failure of the political system in involving a substantial fraction of the tens of millions of nonvoters is likely to determine the future of the country. This proposition goes to the heart of the struggle of the American people for democratic self-realization.

In spite of the fact that there have been a number of get-out-the-vote movements, it is obvious that no serious measures have been taken to bring the forty million into the political system, nothing half so serious as the enactment of a uniform national elections law, for example.

Why has so little been done? Perhaps we shall be near to the truth if we say that little has been done because the question is too important, too hot to be handled. It is by a wide margin the most important feature of the whole system, the key to understanding the composition of American politics. Anyone who finds out how to involve the forty million in American politics will run the country for a generation.

Unquestionably, the addition of forty million voters (or any major fraction of them) would make a tremendous difference. The least that the forty million might do to the political system would be to enhance tremendously the authority of the majority.

The fatuous get-out-the-vote movement conducted through the mass media at election time is a classical instance of the ambivalence of American attitudes toward the problem. The mass-communications industry is precisely the least effective instrument for changing the voting habits of nonparticipants probably because the limitations of the mass-communications system are much like the limitations of the political system.

An attack on the problem of nonvoting calls for a new kind of thinking about politics. What is required to enlarge the political community? A substantial change in public policy might do it. The inference is that the forty million are not likely to become interested in the political system as it is. What the sixty million quarrel about evidently does not excite the forty million. In other words, the forty million can be made to participate only in a new kind of political system based on new cleavages and *about* something new. It is impossible to involve the forty million or any major fraction of them short of a large-scale change in the agenda of politics. What kind of offer do we have to make to get the abstainers into the system?

The problem is serious because the forty million are the soft underbelly of the system. The segment of the population which is least involved or most convinced that the system is loaded against it is the most likely point of subversion. This is the *sickness* of democracy.

The key to the problem is to be found in the nature of public policy and the organization of public support for policy. To put it another way, political support for a major shift of policy can only be found outside the present political system.

It is profoundly characteristic of the behavior of the more fortunate strata of the community that responsibility for widespread nonparticipation is attributed wholly to the ignorance, indifference, and shiftlessness of the people. This has always been the rationalization used to justify the exclusion of the lower classes from any political system. There is a better explanation. Abstention reflects the suppression of the options and alternatives that reflect the needs of the nonparticipants. It is not necessarily true that the people with the greatest needs participate in politics most actively. *Whoever decides what the game is about decides also who can get into the game.* If the political system is dominated by the cleavage AB, what can the people who want another alignment (CD) do? One thing they may do is to stop voting.

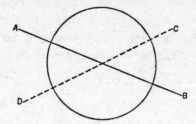

An examination of the social structure of the disfranchised lends support to the foregoing proposition. Who are the forty million? Every study of the subject supports the conclusion that nonvoting is a characteristic of the poorest, least well-established, least educated stratum of the community. Unquestionably, an expansion of the scope of the system would bring a new kind of voter into the community and would change the balance of forces.

The question is: Has the quarrel that underlies American politics been so defined that it excludes a major segment of the nation from the political system?[2]

What is the difference between voters and nonvoters? It is relatively easy to show that the *voters* are more involved in the community than the nonvoters. The voters are better educated, better off, and they belong to more organizations than nonvoters. Voting has something to do with the way in which large areas of need and interest are excluded from the political system.

If the distinction between the forty million and the sixty million is as important as it seems to be, there ought to be some evidence, aside from the voting habits of the people, to support this conclusion. Voting is not an isolated social phenomenon; it is a part of the social condition of the people. There are some general grounds for supposing that the

economic community is divided in about the same way the
political community is divided.

It is surprising how often magnitudes of the general proportions of sixty million appear in American social and economic statistics.

Scope of the Community

Telephone subscribers (1953)	48,056,308
Newspaper circulation (daily, English language, 1953)	54,472,286
Households (1953)	46,828,000
Employment (1959)	62,700,000
Old Age Survivors (insurance coverage, 1954)	69,200,000
Income Tax Returns (1951)	55,042,597
Homes with radio sets (1954)	50,000,000
Automobile registrations (1953)	56,279,864
Television sets (1954)	33,000,000
Votes cast in 1956 election	61,550,918

Without pressing the argument unduly because the statistics are obviously not consistent, does not the recurrence of
these magnitudes suggest that the effective social and economic community may be about as large as the political
community?

The data might seem more significant if they were invert-
ed. It is probably not terribly far from the truth to say that
the forty million nonvoters can be matched by comparable
numbers of adult nonsubscribers to daily newspapers, adult
nonowners of automobiles, adult nonhouseholders, etc. In
other words, there is some basis for thinking that the scope
of the political system is about the same as that of the mass-
communications audience, the automobile market, the tax
system, the social security system, or the market for toothpaste.

Loosely, perhaps we have a sociopolitical community consisting of about sixty million newspaper readers, job holders, income-tax payers, automobile owners, householders, and voters. On the other hand, we have about forty million adults in the community who are less likely to possesss these tokens of participation and status. Crudely the scope of the political community corresponds to the social facts of life. If the *political* distinction between voters and nonvoters corresponds to a social distinction between broadly the same segments of the community, it is the most important datum about the political system, much more important than the distinction between Republicans and Democrats.

The social system makes a substantial distinction between those who have relatively more and those who have relatively less. This is the bias of the system. Have we misconceived the real cleavage in the community? Perhaps the significant division is not between the rich and the poor as these terms are commonly understood, but between people who are more strongly motivated by the economic system and those who are less strongly motivated. Thus an underpaid bank clerk may be greatly excited by the prospect of economic advancement, while a scrub woman working in the same bank may be demoralized and frustrated. The political system is now so preoccupied by *the cleavage within the sixty million* that it has become insensitive to the interests of the largest minority in the world.

Characteristically the processes by which the forty million are excluded from the political system are invisible and imperceptible. Since people are easily overwhelmed or ignored, it takes a special sensitivity to become aware of the needs and experiences of the bottom of the social order. It is one of the great claims of democracy as a moral system that it is able to do this better than any other governmental system, but not all democracies do it equally well.

If politics is thought of as part of the total social experience of people, there must be a great deal about that experience that contradicts the democratic professions of the community.

What is it that people do unconsciously to alienate so large a fraction of the nation? The system operates largely through processes of which people are unaware. Stratification and isolation and segregation are to a great extent the unconscious or semiconscious by-products of the way the social system operates to organize the community. It is not necessary to speak one unkind or ungracious word to keep a poor man out of a rich man's church or college or club or hotel. Anyone familiar with the compulsive standards of dress and play in American schools can understand why the children of the poor drop out of school even when schooling is free.

It is not enough to say that the poor are not hungry and cold. People can suffer from humiliation and degradation as much as from hunger. Poverty is always relative. The point is that *the process is automatic, unconscious, and thoughtless*. People reconcile their democratic faith and their undemocratic behavior by remaining comfortably unaware of the inconsistency of theory and practice.

The sixty million share the same values and play the same game; they participate in politics the way they participate in the life of the community and share in the output of the community. They compete for goods and power. Unfortunately this is not a game in which the whole nation seems to participate.

It is probably fair to say that the existing party system is simply the political organization of the sixty million.

The situation as a whole looks like a good example of the dominance and subordination of conflicts. Since the Democratic-Republican version of the cleavage between government and business has dominated American politics, the submerged millions have found it difficult to get interested in the game.

In view of the foregoing we can start to define the political system all over again: It is the largest, most broadly based, ruling oligarchy in the world, but it is not as inclusive and as broadly based as some other systems.

The contradictions in the political system have produced a party system that is able to exploit some kinds of issues but is much less able to exploit other kinds. Whatever the cause, the present boycott of the political system has brought the political system *very near to something like the limit of tolerance of passive abstention.*

All divisions in the community are maintained at a cost. The existence of a large body of dissociated people is part of the price we pay for the dominance of the cleavage between government and business. This cleavage has tended to freeze the stakes of politics at a point that has never involved the whole community.

Obviously, however, the cleavage between the sixty million and the forty million could be exploited by a new kind of political effort devoted to the development of an array of issues now submerged. On the assumption that the raw materials of a revolution are not likely to remain untouched indefinitely, is it not likely that this is where the future of American politics is to be found?

The root of the problem of nonvoting is to be found in the way in which the alternatives in American politics are defined, the way in which issues get referred to the public, the scale of competition and organization, and above all by *what* issues are developed. The existence of a large nonvoting population provides an insight into the nature of the unresolved historic tensions in the system.

The political system *has never assigned to the elective process a role as overwhelmingly important as that played by British elections.* The political system is not well designed to bring great issues to a head in a national election. Until recently the party alignment was so sharply sectional that the bulk of American voters lived in one-party areas where they had little incentive to vote because they had no choices. A national party system based on national cleavages is only now beginning to emerge, and it may be some time before all Americans have a genuine party choice, even in presidential elections.

Whether or not the rate of political participation will ever be developed on a satisfactory scale depends to a great extent *on the evolution of American policy about politics,* political organization, and the rights of political organizations.

A great multitude of causes languish because the forty million or so nonvoters do not support them at the polls. It staggers the imagination to consider what might happen if the forty million suddenly intervened, for we cannot take it for granted that they would be divided in the same proportions as the sixty million. All political equations would be revised.

All classical concepts of democracy have overestimated the strength and universality of the self-generated impulse of people to participate in the life of the political community. It has been assumed that only legal barriers inhibited the disfranchised. We know better now. The exclusion of people by extralegal processes, by social processes, by the way the political system is organized and structured may be far more effective than the law.

Two major tasks of modern politics suggest that the problem deserves examination. First, politics today must cope with the potentialities and the problems created by annihilation of space. The mobility of modern man makes him a member of more and larger communities than any of his predecessors. Nobody knows what the potentialities of these new communities are. The political processes of large-scale society are unlike those of the old, and the balance of forces is inevitably different.

In the second place, modern politics must deal with a kind of shift of emphasis from the politics of the distribution of benefits to the politics of the apportionment of burdens. The traditional concept of politics (once described as who gets what, when, and how) was invented at a time when the stability and survival of the American community could be so fully taken for granted that it was possible to think about the political process almost exclusively in terms of the acquisitive instinct.

Today our view of politics is greatly modified by the fact that the United States is involved in a titanic struggle for survival. Burdens that were inconceivable a few years ago seem to have become a permanent part of the public function. *The primacy of foreign policy* calls for a new kind of politics involving a wholly new calculus. The government now needs above everything else the steady support of the public, and this support cannot be had without a new scale of public involvement in public life.

A greatly expanded popular base of political participation is the essential condition for public support of the government. This is the modern problem of democratic government. The price of support is participation. The choice is between participation and propaganda, between democratic and dictatorial ways of *changing consent into support, because consent is no longer enough.*

Perhaps the calculation that is going to have the greatest influence on the future of the system is based on the estimate that it is easier to bring a new voter into the system than it is to induce an old partisan to change sides. The expansion of the community is related to the nationalization of politics; the larger the community the more likely it is to be favorable to the admission of new elements, whereas localization has historically been the strategic base for restricting the scope of politics.

The expansion of the participating political community ought to be a major objective of American politics. We ought therefore to elicit the support of those people already in the participating political community who are likely to have the greatest interest in its expansion. We ought to look to the newcomers and the less privileged elements of the population to elicit their support for new programs of public action. In other words, *we ought now to use political means to extend the scope of social and political organization.*

What we need now is public policy about politics.

Notes

1. It has often been pointed out to us that the turnout in parliamentary elections outside of the United States is apt to be about 80 percent, approximately 20 percent higher than it is in the United States. However, American elections are not very much like British elections, to take a European example. An Englishman voting in a general election casts one vote for a single candidate for one office, using a ballot about the size of a government post card. American elections are, on the other hand, extremely complex. Not only do we elect about eight hundred thousand officials but before the elections there are the primaries, and before the primaries, in many jurisdictions, comes periodic personal registration of voters. American voters must cope with fifty systems of election laws. Technical arguments about the exact size of the nonvoting public are not important. It is a large piece of cheese no matter how one slices it.

See Austin Ranney, *The Governing of Men*, New York, 1958, p. 266, for an analysis of American statistics for the 1956 election.

The whole subject is discussed extensively in Robert E. Lane, *Political Life*, Free Press, 1959.

2. "The apathy toward the parties cuts across every ward and income group, but the highest percentage of unenrolled people is to be found in the low-income Catholic wards where those who do indicate party affiliation are largely Democrats. Political inactivity is also revealed in the failure to register to vote. This tendency is deepest in low-income Democratic,

Catholic areas." K. Underwood, *Protestant and Catholic*, Beacon Press, 1957, pp. 295–296.

See also L. Warner and Associates, *Democracy in Jonesville*, Chapters 6, 9, 12.

See Robert E. Lane, *Political Life*, Free Press, 1959, Chapter XVI, for a review of the data about the influence of status on political participation.

7

What Does Change Look Like?

SO far in this book we have been discussing changes in the nature of conflict due 1) to the development or expansion of conflict, the changing scope of the involvement, and 2) to the displacement of subordinate conflicts by dominant conflicts. As long as we deal with conflicts that are not fully established, great fluidity in the political system may result from the fact that conflict is highly contagious and from the circumstance that conflicts compete with each other for a place in the center of the arena.

What happens to conflicts that are so fully developed and established that they cannot be displaced and cannot be resolved?

Is the political system stalemated by cleavages so firmly established that they seem to divide the community permanently? The answer to this question is vitally important because it tells us whether or not the system is dynamic or stagnant.

It might be well to observe at the outset some differences between resolvable conflicts and unresolvable conflicts. In an unresolvable conflict neither side can be overwhelmed, both sides are able and willing to continue the struggle indefinitely, and neither side can escape the necessity of continuing the struggle.

What we are really saying is that an unresolvable conflict implies the existence of an equilibrium. It follows that the permanent built-in conflicts in our society can be best understood in terms of the politics of equilibriums. The question is, therefore: What happens when the political system is dominated by the need to maintain an equilibrium? What does an equilibrium look like? Is an equilibrium only another word for a stalemate, or is it compatible with the existence of a dynamic political system?

A good example of a well-developed conflict that seems to be unresolvable is the conflict between government and business. This conflict is built into a system that is both democratic and capitalistic. Both of these antagonists are powerful and resourceful and resolute; both are well-intrenched, and both have substantially unlimited staying power. Has this conflict stalemated the political system?

There is a great abundance of evidence to show that the unresolved and unresolvable conflict of government and business has not deadlocked the system or checked the process of change. It is almost impossible to exaggerate the changes that have been made in the government and in public policy in spite of the tensions described here.

For example, it is impossible to say when or where it happened, but the attitude of Americans toward their government has undergone a profound change in the course of our national history. For more than a century we have been *giving the government to the people* until the people have come to believe us; they think that they own it. The public no longer identifies itself with the House of Representatives as its special agency in the government, as it ought to in constitutional theory. Americans now think that their title covers the whole government, lock, stock, and barrel, not merely a piece of it. Like all great proprietors they are not interested in details or excuses; they want *results.* In other words, *they believe that they have a general power over the government as a whole and not merely some power within the government.*

This is a profoundly revolutionary change in the concept of power which cannot be fitted into anything written in the *Federalist Papers* or in the literature of constitutional law. It is a change not brought about by an act of Congress, a decision of the Supreme Court, a constitutional convention, or a constitutional amendment, but by a kind of general consent. Somewhere along the line the owners of the government decided to read the Constitution as if it were a democratic document. This is unquestionably the most important interpretation of the Constitution in our history. It can be understood only on the assumption that the general expectations of the proprietors of the government have been changed profoundly.

Take some other examples. What has become of the view widely held a generation ago that the treaty provisions of the Constitution were unworkable? Or, what is the real status of the doctrine of limited government today? The government of the United States is now a very powerful organization, perhaps the most powerful organization in the history of the world. There is nothing inevitable about the survival of the United States, but if it fails it will not be for lack of power or money.

While we were looking the other way, the government of the United States became a global operation a decade or two ago. The budget is about two hundred fifty times as large as it was seventy years ago. If you multiply the diameter of a baseball by two hundred fifty very suddenly, you have an explosion. Is it possible to understand American politics without considering the regime a going concern? What kind of operation has the government of the United States become? The changes in the regime are so great that one might well ask whether or not our theoretical equipment is adequate for the comprehension of what has happened.

In a purely formal sense we can say that the government of the United States is the same one that was established in 1789—in about the same way in which Henry Ford's bicycle repair shop is the same as the Ford Motor Company today.

The achievements of the regime are all the more remarkable in view of the fact that we have a governmental apparatus that looks for all the world like a Rube Goldberg cartoon. The theme of a generation of writers on American public affairs has been the unworkability of the machinery of government. It would be difficult to find anywhere in the world a gap that is wider than that between the generally pessimistic and defeatist tone of the literature of American government and politics on the one hand and the performance of the regime on the other.

Evidently the unresolved tension between government and business has not inhibited the process of change.

We might make greater progress toward an understanding of the dynamics of American politics if we ignored the complexities of the governmental structure and began to examine the struggle for power in a new dimension. Is it not likely that the separation of powers reflects obsolete conflicts that have little relevance to the contemporary struggle? The whole of the ancient British social structure around which the separation of powers was built originally has long since passed into the limbo. The deepest cleavages in the modern world are no longer those that turn the President against Congress or the courts. We get confused because we cling to the ancient battlements long after the armies have abandoned them and the conflict has moved to new battlefields. The scene of conflict has shifted so greatly that the government itself is now involved in a wholly new dimension of conflict. The unresolvable conflicts are no longer car-

ried on *within* the old governmental structure; the new
conflicts characteristically involve the whole government in
struggles with powers wholly *outside* the government. Today the government itself competes for power.

It may be useful to examine two of the greatest of modern, built-in, unresolvable conflicts to see what light they
shed on this discussion.

The conflict of government and business illustrates the
new dimensions of the dominant tensions. It requires no
demonstration to support the proposition that the relation
between government and business has given rise to some of
the greatest tensions in modern life and that these tensions
tend to dominate the political system.

Business so dominates the nongovernmental world that it
looks very much like a power system able to compete with
the government itself. Once upon a time the church was the
principal nongovernmental institution; today it is business.
Nowadays business plays so great a role in the community, it
has developed so great an organization, has such vast resources that it is inevitably the principal focus of power outside of the government, a focus of power that challenges the
supremacy of government in the modern community. As a
matter of fact, the relations of government and business
largely determine the character of the regime. Seen this
way the struggle for power is largely a confrontation of two
major power systems, government and business.

The very magnitude of the two systems makes it impossible for them to be indifferent to each other. Control of the
vast aggregates of wealth involved in the corporate structure of modern business is a power mobilization of such proportions that it is virtually forced to compete with government. In terms of almost any conceivable definition of power, business deserves to be called a power system of the first
order. If money is power, obviously business has so much

money that it must be powerful. If we have difficulty in thinking of business as a competitor with government, it is only because we have been educated to believe that competition with the government is unthinkable.

The rivalry of government and business is not abated by the fact that the antagonists are interdependent and inseparable (everybody belongs to both empires). Nor is the conflict made less real by the fact that it is never fully avowed as a power struggle. The quarrel dominates the political system precisely because it is not a war of extermination; this is what makes the conflict unresolvable. The political system has had a long time to organize itself around this quarrel.

The mixture of capitalism and democracy in the American regime presupposes tension. Tension is increased by the fact that power in the two systems is aggregated on radically different principles. The political system is broadly equalitarian, *numbers* are important in politics. The whole emphasis of the law and tradition of the political system is designed to invite the widest possible participation in the process.

On the other hand, the economic system is exclusive; it fosters a high degree of inequality and invites concentration of power. There is, moreover, a strong dogmatic base for the assumption that the *public* responsibilities of business are limited. The bias of the two systems is profoundly different.

Imagine a political system in which votes are bought and sold freely in the open market, a system in which it is taken for granted that people will buy all the votes they can afford and use their power to get more money in order to buy more votes, so that a single magnate might easily outvote a whole city. Imagine a situation in which elections have become a mere formality because one or a few individuals are owners of a controlling number of votes. Suppose that nine tenths of the members of the community are unable to exert any appreciable influence. Suppose, moreover, that the minority is entitled to very little information about what is being done. That is what the political system would be like if it were run the way business is run.

It is unlikely that two such power systems as government and business could inhabit the same space without collision. If ever a contest was built into a regime, the conflict between government and business is it.

The dualism of government and business in the American system did not arise by chance or mischance. It is a romantic misreading of history to suppose that Americans first established a pristine democracy which later was corrupted by the money power. Rather, American democracy was an early attempt to split the political power from the economic power. This is the great American experiment. In the long story of western civilization the union of economic and political power has been the rule, not the exception, i.e., the owners of economic power were also the owners of the government. One of the first great breaches in this ancient system was made by the American attempt to divorce the two powers. Indeed, it was possible to democratize the political system without a bloody social revolution because Americans invented a working model for splitting the two kinds of power.

Why have Americans failed to understand the importance of this development? Our view of history has been distorted by the compulsion to interpret our past in terms of traditional concepts of popular sovereignty. In view of the traditional definition of democracy it was necessary to invent the myth that the people seized all power at the time of the American Revolution. Next, it became necessary to suppose that the idyllic democratic system established at the end of the eighteenth century has been subverted by the rise of big business.

A recognition of the dualism of government and business provides a much better interpretation of American history. The American Revolution was an incident in a conflict that is still going on. *The function of democracy has been to provide the public with a second power system, an alternative power system, which can be used to counterbalance the economic power.* For this reason, it was necessary to create a broad democratic base of the political system. This is why government and business so often seem to be alternative ways of doing the same things. If government by business now seems intolerable, it is because we have developed new concepts of the functions of government. There is so much reckless talk about the relations of government and business that we ought to make an effort to bear in mind the point that the divorce of the two power systems is perhaps the greatest American political achievement.

Politics, as we now understand it, developed as a consequence of the separation of the economic and the political powers, just as politics in an earlier period revolved about the separation of church and state. The rise of modern American politics is related to the growth of political parties which were able to capture the government while leaving control of the economy largely untouched.

The separation of the political and economic powers was facilitated by the breakup of mercantilism and the rise of *laissez-faire* concepts of public policy at about the same time that democratic political ideas gained wide popular acceptance. The democratic movement was so exclusively political that most of us have difficulty trying to imagine what the democratization of the economy would look like.

The division of the political and economic powers was bound to create a new kind of government because it gave the government a new assignment. On the other hand, the economic interpretation of politics, a very old interpretation of politics, broadly ignores what has happened to the political system in the past century. If business really dominated the government, how long would a public discussion of the relations of government and business have been possible?

What is the nature of the public interest in this equilibrium of government and business? First, *the public does not seem to be very much interested in a resolution of the conflict*. It does not like any of the standard resolutions such as fascism or communism. Whatever the legal and theoretical powers of the government may be, it has never received a mandate to abolish the capitalist system. On the other hand, government by business seems intolerable. There are urgent reasons for the perpetuation of the conflict. Paul Appleby has said:

> It may be unfortunate, but it is nevertheless a fact that because of factors beyond its control no industry can realize its own social aspirations. It is also true that no industry can regard public interest equally with industrial interest. That cannot be its function; it must have a different and narrower one. Governments exist precisely for the reason that there is a need to have special persons in society charged with the function of promoting and protecting the public interest.[1]

In some ways *the public interest resides in the no man's land between government and business*. The public wants to preserve its options, the kinds of options it would lose if either the fascist or communist resolutions were adopted.

There is something about the government that makes it grow when it is attacked. The public likes *competitive power systems*. It wants both democracy and a high standard of living and thinks it can have both provided it can maintain a dynamic equilibrium between the democratic and the capitalist elements in the regime. The public is willing to try to get along with the capitalist system provided that it can maintain alongside it a democratic political system powerful enough to police it.

What has the equilibrium done to American government? It has meant that big business has had to be matched at all points by what Paul Appleby calls big democracy. Every change in the organization, technology, and scope of the economy has had to be matched by parallel changes in the organization of political power. The point is that governmental change becomes possible when it is necessary to preserve the equilibrium. Once we understand this proposition a host of other data fall into place because the necessities of the equilibrium determine what can and what cannot be done.

If we start from the proposition that competitive power relations are the key to politics, we might have less difficulty in understanding why things have changed so rapidly. The key concept is that competitive situations survive only as long as the competitors are able to maintain a kind of parity of the capacity to compete. Anything that disturbs this parity affects all of the contestants with devastating intensity.

People value government because it is the only device that is able to protect them against competing power systems of which they do not approve wholly, power systems they fear or cannot control. The way the government acts is related to the way people react to nongovernmental power systems. Governments feed on these reactions. The irresistible stimulus is the growth of the competitors. People value government not because it is omnipotent but because the world is a dangerous place in which to live. If we want to understand what is happening to government, we must look at what its rivals are doing, not merely at the formal governmental institutions. Paraphrasing a statement made in another connection long ago, we might say about the government of the United States that we love it for the enemies it has made.

Only the strong can compete because the scale of competition is always determined by the scale and force of the antagonists. A competitive situation can continue only in something like an equilibrium. The law of competition is therefore that each competitor must match the scale of operations of his principal competitors to survive. Spelled out in more detail this analysis means that students of politics must be concerned about the equilibriums implicit in the unresolvable conflicts imbedded in the regime.

In a society that is highly sensitive to changes in the equilibrium anything that touches the seamless web of power relations involves everything else. The most significant difference between the private domain and the public domain is that in private conflict the strong prevail whereas in public domain the weak combine for self-defense.

Everything that might be said about the impact on the government of changes in the economy ought to be multiplied many times when we consider the effect of changes in the world balance of power on American government. The point of this discussion is that the unresolvable conflicts built into the regime do not produce a stalemate; the equilibrium is dynamic.

As a matter of fact, the unresolvable conflicts have not deadlocked American politics for another reason: The cleavages produced are inconsistent and contradictory. It follows that each can be used to bring tremendous pressure on the other. Movement within the political system is related therefore to the kind of leverage that two inconsistent cleavages can exert on each other.

The equilibriums are dynamic because they are maintained amid the fantastic growth of all competitors for power. The government is irrevocably committed to keeping up

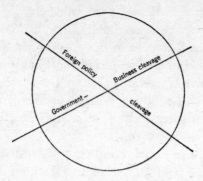

with all the Joneses, at home and abroad. The scale of organization and the locus of power within the government respond predictably to any change in the power, technology, or scope of operations of its principal antagonists.

Competition is the life of government. To destroy the equilibrium is to destroy one government and to create another. What government *must* do and *can* do is determined by what happens to the competition. The chief factor in the governmental revolution of our times has been the rise of enormous new power concentrations abroad and at home which have destroyed the old balance of power and forced us to make a stupendous effort to restore the equilibrium.

The sense of urgency behind the drive to preserve the equilibrium is so strong and the compensatory changes in the government are made so easily that we are hardly aware of them. The reaction is almost automatic. That is how it happens that most of us do not know that we have created a new government in the past three decades. We never decided to create a new government. We thought that we were merely rallying around to preserve the status quo.

We have had difficulty preceiving change because we have looked for the wrong kind of conflict (conflict *within* the government) and have underestimated the extent to which *the government itself as a whole* has been in conflict with other power systems. When the government as a whole is in conflict with other powers, conflict within the government is subordinated, no matter how earnestly we pretend that this is not so.

The use of unresolvable conflicts to keep alive the alternatives within the political system is well within the American tradition. The conflicts of church and state and of the king and barons are closely related to the origins of liberty, because the little people profited by the divisions among the powerful. *In the United States in the middle of the twentieth century the new equilibrium of government and business has been made possible by the rise of modern democracy and modern industrialism* which created the base for a new division of powers. The erosion of the checks and balances in the United States Constitution in modern times has been due to the fact that there has been a shift in the dominant cleavages in our society. A great part of the confusion of our times results from the fact that we are substituting a new separation of powers for the old one.

Nor is this the first time that we have revised the alignments of forces institutionalized in the Constitution. The British Glorious Revolution Constitution was a trap designed to catch a king. A century later this trap was imported by Americans in spite of the fact that we had no king.

Democracy as we know it today depends on the way in which the political and the economic powers are played off against each other, the way we steer a course between dominance and subservience. We need not be dismayed to find that business is powerful. Power is inherent in modern business organization. The object of the game is not to destroy business power but to match it with governmental power.

The foregoing line of thought implies a notion about the function of modern government. One way of describing this function is to say that government is organized for the preservation of the familiar landscape. For this reason we do not like unilateral solutions. This feeling has something to do with our sense of equality, justice, and security. On the other hand we do not object to the greatest changes imaginable as long as they are general and everything changes at the same time and changes to approximately the same extent.

It is remarkable how little opposition is aroused by general changes that affect us like the pressure of an atmosphere. How easily we become accustomed to changes that have become universalized! What might the automobile have done to our society if it had become the exclusive possession of a privileged class? Or what would have happened if selective service had not been made universal? Changes in the *relative position* of things are painful.

How can changes in the modern political scene be identified? Superficially, they can't be seen at all. Change is possible in part because it is often imperceptible, because it is usually done in the name of preserving the status quo.

Note

1. *Big Democracy*, Alfred A. Knopf, New York, 1945, p. 5.

8

The Semisovereign People

THE line of thought developed in the preceding chapters of this book ought to shed some light on the meaning of democracy. The role of the people in the political system is determined largely by the conflict system, for it is conflict that involves the people in politics and the nature of conflict determines the nature of the public involvement.

The idea that the people are involved in politics by the contagion of conflict does not resemble the classical definition of democracy as "government by the people." The difference between the idea of popular "involvement" in conflict and the idea that people actually "govern" is great enough to invite a re-examination of the classical theory of democracy. Does the consideration of the place of conflict in a free political system open up the way for a redefinition of democracy in modern terms?

Whether we know it or not, all speculation about American politics rests on some image of democracy. The literature on the subject has been so permeated by democratic and pseudodemocratic ideas that it is impossible to understand what we are talking about unless we isolate and identify these ideas and try to distinguish between the democratic and antidemocratic elements in them.

126

The devotion of the American public to the democratic ideal is so overwhelming that we test everything by it. It is surprising to find, therefore, that political philosophers have had remarkable difficulty in defining the word *democracy*. As a matter of fact, the failure to produce a good working definition of democracy is responsible for a great part of the confusion in the literature of politics. An examination of the problem might be worth while, therefore.

The classical definition of democracy as government by the people is predemocratic in its origins, based on notions about democracy developed by philosophers who never had an opportunity to see an operating democratic system. Predemocratic theorists assumed that the people would take over the conduct of public affairs in a democracy and administer the government to their own advantage as simply as landowners administer their property for their own profit. Under the historical circumstances this oversimplification is easy to understand. There is less excuse for the failure of modern scholars to re-examine the traditional definition critically in the light of modern experience.[1]

One consequence of our reliance on old definitions is that the modern American does not look at democracy before he defines it; he defines it first and then is confused by what he sees. In spite of the fact that the ancients made some astonishing miscalculations about democracy as an operating system, their authority is so great that the traditional definition is perpetuated in the textbooks and governs our thinking in the entire area.

The confusion of ideas about democracy looks like a job for the political scientists. What we need is a modern definition of democracy explaining the facts of life of the operating political system, a definition that distinguishes between the democratic and antidemocratic elements in the developing contemporary political situation. The great deficiency of American democracy is intellectual, the lack of a good, usable definition. A good definition might shed a flood of light on modern politics; it might clarify a thousand muddy concepts and might help us understand where we are going and what we want. It might even help us get rid of the impossible imperatives that haunt the literature of the subject and give everyone a sense of guilt. We need to reexamine the chasm between theory and practice because it is at least as likely that the ideal is wrong as it is that the reality is bad. Certainly our chances of getting democracy and keeping it would be better if we made up our minds about what it is.[2]

Perhaps as good a point as any at which to test our ideas about democracy is in the general area of public opinion research. This research is based on the assumption that public opinion plays a great role in a democracy. Lurking in the background is the notion that the people actually do govern.

What image of democracy leads us to assign a central place in political theory to public opinion? The question is: Can we define the role of public opinion in a democracy before we make up our minds about what democracy is? Before we invest the energies of a generation of political scientists in public opinion research, would it not be wise to make an attempt to *test* the validity of the underlying propositions about the relations of public opinion to what is happening in the world about us?[3]

It requires no research to demonstrate that it is difficult to relate the copybook maxims about democracy to the operating political system. If we start with the common definition of democracy (as government by the people), it is hard to avoid some extremely pessimistic conclusions about the feasibility of democracy in the modern world, for it is impossible to reconcile traditional concepts of what ought to happen in a democracy with the fact that an amazingly large number of people do not seem to know very much about what is going on. The significance of this kind of popular ignorance depends on what we think democracy is.

Research might have enlightened us much more than it has if the researchers had taken the time to formulate an operating democratic theory. It is hard to see how anyone can formulate a satisfactory theory of public opinion without meeting this problem head on. What is the function of the public in a modern democracy? What does the public have to know? The failure to understand how the public intervenes in the political process, what the public can be expected to do, what it cannot do, how questions get referred to the public has led to quantities of remarkably pointless speculation. How do we find out what we are looking for?

The reader can make a test of the basic proposition for himself by spending some time examining the massive compilation of polls in *Public Opinion, 1935–1946* made by Hadley Cantril and Mildred Strunk.[4] While this compilation, twelve hundred pages of it, is no longer fully representative of the work done by scholars today, it has one incomparable advantage to students of politics—*the polls were taken at least thirteen years ago.* After a lapse of several years we are in a position to ask: How nearly do the data turned up in these polls correspond with what actually happened? For some reason when one now looks at this body of data, it seems to lack reality. If the assumption is that public opinion is important because it determines public policy, a comparison of the polls and the history of the decade raises a flood of doubts. How much difference did the opinions measured in these polls actually make?

It is necessary only to look at the polls on birth control, the budget, capital punishment, divorce, employee representation schemes, the excess-profits tax, free speech, income limitation, industrial and labor relations, small busi-

ness, socialized medicine, race relations, government ownership of public utilities, neutrality, and the territorial expansion of the United States to realize that public opinion
about specific issues does not necessarily govern the course
of public policy.

The point of this discussion is that political research is
never better than the theory of politics on which it is based.
The theory of the polls is essentially simplistic, based on a
tremendously exaggerated notion of the immediacy and urgency of the connection of public opinion and events. The
result is that sometimes we seem to be interviewing the fish
in the sea to find out what the birds in the heavens are
doing.

What would it be worth to students of politics if by some
miracle they could know precisely what everybody in the
country was thinking at twelve noon last Friday? Probably
very little. We are in trouble because we are confused about
what is supposed to happen in a democracy.

The image implicit in the schoolbook definition of democracy is that of a mass of people who think about politics the
way a United States senator might think about it. In this
image public opinion has great consequences; what the people think has a compulsive impact on what the government
does. It follows that the scholar ought to begin his studies at
the grass roots.

The great difficulty here is theoretical, not technical; it
concerns the assumptions made about the role of the people
in a democracy. The unstated premise in a multitude of
polls is that the people really do decide what the government does on something like a day-to-day basis. This assumption implies a definition of democracy. How can we
get hold of the subject if we do not deal with this definition?

A hundred million voters have a staggering number of opinions about an incredible number of subjects. Under what circumstances do these opinions become important?

The problem is one of definition. What is the role of the public in a democracy? What have we a right to expect of the public? Is it possible to reformulate the question in terms of democratic concepts other than the primitive notions derived from the ancients?

Apparently the attitude of the public is far more permissive than the hortatory, high-pressure, special-interest school of theorists thinks it ought to be. The tendency of the literature of politics is to place a tremendous premium on the role of the interested and to treat indifference as a mortal sin, but the reluctance of the public to press its opinions on the government concerning a great multitude of issues is really not as bad a thing as we may have been led to think; it is a mark of reasonableness and common sense. The public is far too sensible to attempt to play the preposterous role assigned to it by the theorists. We have tended to undervalue this attitude because we have labored under an illusion about democracy.

We become cynical about democracy because the public does not act the way the simplistic definition of democracy says that it should act, or we try to whip the public into doing things it does not want to do, is unable to do, and has too much sense to do. The crisis here is not a crisis in democracy but a crisis in theory.

The importance of democratic theory is demonstrated by the way in which students of public opinion have neglected what is perhaps their most important discovery, the discovery of the "don't knows," the very large category of people who are willing to confess that they do not seem to know very much about what is going on in the government. The tendency has been to ignore this discovery because it does not fit very conveniently into our preconceptions about democracy and the democratic process. The "don't knows" are treated as unfortunate exceptions to the democratic proposition about whom we prefer not to think. This is remarkable because ignorance is an ancient condition of the human race. The significance of this widespread ignorance about public affairs depends largely on what we think democracy is.

One implication of public opinion studies ought to be resisted by all friends of freedom and democracy; the implication that democracy is a failure because the people are too ignorant to answer intelligently all the questions asked by the pollsters. This is a professorial invention for imposing professorial standards on the political system and deserves to be treated with extreme suspicion. Only a pedagogue would suppose that the people must pass some kind of examination to qualify for participation in a democracy. Who, after all, are these self-appointed censors who assume that they are in a position to flunk the whole human race? Their attitude would be less presumptuous if they could come up with a list of things that people must know. Who can say what the man on the street must know about public affairs? The whole theory of knowledge underlying these assumptions is pedantic. Democracy was made for the people, not the people for democracy. Democracy is something for ordinary people, a political system designed to be sensitive to the needs of ordinary people regardless of whether or not the pedants approve of them.

It is an outrage to attribute the failures of American democracy to the ignorance and stupidity of the masses. The most disastrous shortcomings of the system have been those of the intellectuals whose concepts of democracy have been amazingly rigid and uninventive. The failure of the intellectuals is dangerous because it creates confusion in high places. Unless the intellectuals can produce a better theory of politics than they have, it is possible that we shall abolish democracy before we have found out what it is!

The intellectuals have done very little to get us out of the theoretical trap created by the disparity between the demands made on the public by the common definition of democracy and the capacity of the public to meet these demands.[5] The embarrassment results from the reluctance of intellectuals to develop a definition that describes what really happens in a democracy.

The whole mass of illusions discussed in the foregoing paragraph arises from a confusion of ideas about what people need to know, what the role of the public in a democracy is, how the public functions in a democracy.

If we assume that the people "govern," it follows that the governing majority ought to know more than any majority has ever known or ever could know. This is the *reductio ad absurdum* of democratic theory. We cannot get out of the dilemma by (1) making a great effort to educate everyone to the point where they know enough to make these decisions or (2) by restricting participation to the people who do know all about these matters. The first is impossible. The second is absurd because *no one* knows enough to govern by this standard. The trouble is that we have defined democracy in such a way that we are in danger of putting ourselves out of business.

There is no escape from the problem of ignorance, because *nobody knows enough to run the government.* Presidents, senators, governors, judges, professors, doctors of philosophy, editors, and the like are only a little less ignorant than the rest of us. Even an expert is a person who chooses to be ignorant about many things so that he may know all about one.

The whole theory of knowledge underlying these concepts of democracy is false—it proves too much. It proves not only that democracy is impossible; it proves equally that life itself is impossible. Everybody has to accommodate himself to the fact that he deals daily with an incredible number of matters about which he knows very little. This is true of all aspects of life, not merely of politics.

The compulsion to know everything is the road to insanity.

People are able to survive in the modern world by learning to distinguish between what they must know and what they do not need to know. We get a clue to the solution of the problem when we begin to realize that it is not necessary to be an automotive engineer to buy an automobile or to be an obstetrician in order to have a baby. Our survival depends on our ability to judge things by their results and our ability to establish relations of confidence and responsibility so that we can take advantage of what other people know. We could not live in modern society if we did not place confidence daily in a thousand ways in pharmacists, surgeons, pilots, bank clerks, engineers, plumbers, technicians, lawyers, civil servants, accountants, courts, telephone operators, craftsmen, and a host of others. We pass judgment on the most complex mechanisms on the basis of the *results* they produce. Economists, trying to explain the operation of the economy, use a political expression when they speak of the "sovereignty of the consumer" precisely because they realize that it is not necessary to know how to *make* a television set in order to buy one intelligently. Democracy is like nearly everything else we do; it is a form of collaboration of ignorant people and experts.

Primitive democratic theorists never tire of telling us that democracy was designed to work in New England town meetings, not in a modern national state. The analysis is

fatuous. We might as well attempt to return to a handicraft
economy. The crisis is a purely theoretical one because operating democratic political systems have in fact already accomplished what is theoretically impossible and are doing it
every day. It is only the theory that has broken down. The
problem of modern democracy is the problem of learning to
live in the modern world.

We can find our way through the maze if we learn to
distinguish between different kinds of knowledge, between
what amateurs know and what professionals know, between
what generalists know and what specialists know. The problem is not how 180 million Aristotles can run a democracy,
but how we can organize a political community of 180 million ordinary people so that it remains sensitive to their
needs. This is a problem of *leadership, organization, alternatives, and systems of responsibility and confidence.* The
emphasis is on the role of leadership and organization in a
democracy, not on the spontaneous generation of something at the grass roots. If we approach the problem from
this side, it does not look impossible. The achievements of
the American regime are tremendous, but they have been
brought about in spite of the theoretical illusions under
which we have labored.

The people are involved in public affairs by the conflict
system. Conflicts open up questions for public intervention.
Out of conflict the alternatives of public policy arise. Conflict is the occasion for political organization and leadership.
In a free political system it is difficult to avoid public involvement in conflict; the ordinary, regular operations of
the government give rise to controversy, and controversy is
catching.

The beginning of wisdom in democratic theory is to distinguish between the things the people can do and the
things the people cannot do. The worst possible disservice

that can be done to the democratic cause is to attribute to
the people a mystical, magical omnipotence which takes no
cognizance of what very large numbers of people cannot do
by the sheer weight of numbers. At this point the common
definition of democracy has invited us to make fools of ourselves.

What 180 million people can do spontaneously, on their
own initiative, is not much more than a locomotive can do
without rails. The public is like a very rich man who is unable to supervise closely all of his enterprise. His problem is
to learn how to compel his agents to define his options.

What we are saying is that conflict, competition, leadership, and organization are the essence of democratic politics. Inherent in the operations of a democracy are special
conditions which permit large numbers of people to   function.

The problem is how to organize the political system so as
to make the best possible use of the power of the public in
view of its limitations. A popular decision bringing into focus the force of public support requires a tremendous effort
to define the alternatives, to organize the discussion and
mobilize opinion. The government and the political organizations are in the business of manufacturing this kind of
alternatives.

What has been said here has not been said to belittle the
power of the people but to shed some light on what it is.
The power of the people is not made less by the fact that it
cannot be used for trivial matters. The whole world can be
run on the basis of a remarkably small number of decisions.
The power of the people in a democracy depends on the
importance of the decisions made by the electorate, not on
the *number* of decisions they make. Since the adoption of
the Constitution the party in power has been turned out by
the opposition party fourteen times, and in about six of

these instances the consequences have been so great that we could not understand American history without taking account of them.

The most important thing about any democratic regime is the *way* in which it *uses* and exploits popular sovereignty, what questions it refers to the public for decision or guidance, how it refers them to the public, how the alternatives are defined and how it respects the limitations of the public. A good democratic system protects the public against the demand that it do impossible things. The unforgivable sin of democratic politics is to dissipate the power of the public by putting it to trivial uses. What we need is a movement for the conservation of the political resources of the American people.

Above everything, *the people are powerless if the political enterprise is not competitive.* It is the competition of political organizations that provides the people with the opportunity to make a choice. Without this opportunity popular sovereignty amounts to nothing.

The common definition of democracy may be harmless if it is properly understood, but the fact is that it is very commonly misunderstood. It would be more imaginative to say that some things we now are actually doing are democratic even though they do not fit the traditional definition. Definitions of democracy since the time of Aristotle have been made on the assumption that the "many" in a democracy do the same things that the "one" does in a monarchy and the "few" do in an aristocracy. But obviously the shift from the "one" to the "many" is not merely a change in the number of people participating in power but *a change in the way the power is exercised.* The 180 million cannot do what a single ruler can do. This is not because the 180 million are stupid or ignorant but because it is physically impossible for 180 million to act the way one acts. In the interests of clarity and the survival of the political system we need a definition of democracy that recognizes the limitations that nature imposes on large numbers.

A working definition must capitalize on the limitations of the people as well as their powers. We do this when we say that liberty and leadership are the greatest of democratic concepts. *Democracy is a competitive political system in which competing leaders and organizations define the alternatives of public policy in such a way that the public can participate in the decision-making process.* The initiative in this political system is to be found largely in the government or in the opposition. The people profit by this system, but they cannot, by themselves, do the work of the system. We have already had a great deal of experience with this kind of system. Is it not about time that we begin to recognize its democratic implications?

Conflict, competition, organization, leadership, and responsibility are the ingredients of a working definition of democracy. Democracy is a political system in which the people have a choice among the alternatives created by competing political organizations and leaders. The advantage of this definition over the traditional definition is that it is *operational*, it describes something that actually happens. It describes something feasible. It does not make impossible demands on the public. Moreover, it describes a going democratic concern whose achievements are tremendous.

The involvement of the public in politics is a natural outgrowth of the kind of conflict that almost inevitably arises in a free society. The exploitation of this situation by responsible political leaders and organizations is the essence of democracy; the socialization of conflict is the essential democratic process.

Notes

1. What the Greek philosophers had to say about Athens, a city-state having a population of thirty thousand, three fourths of whom were slaves, has very little to do with democracy in a nation of 180 million.

2. There have been many attempts to define democracy. This is not the place to make a compilation of these definitions. The attack here is on the most pervasive and widely accepted common definition of democracy as "government by the people." At the same time that we have defined democracy as something unattainable, we have made democracy one of the most emotion-charged words in our civilization. This is the impossible imperative which threatens to entrap all of us.

3. See Bernard Berelson, "Democratic Theory and Public Opinion," pp. 107 ff., in Eulau, Eldersveld, and Janowitz, *Political Behavior*, Free Press, Glencoe, Illinois, 1956, for a good statement of what seems to be the concept of democracy prevailing among students of public opinion; it illustrates very well how much students of public opinion have been influenced by the common definition of democracy.

See also Burdick's criticism of Berelson's ideas in Burdick and Brodbeck, *American Voting Behavior*, Free Press, 1959, pp. 136 ff.

4. Princeton University Press, 1951.

5. So highly respected a modern theorist as Francis W. Coker deals with this subject in one short paragraph and disposes of the matter by quoting Bryce's definition of democracy as "majority rule." *Recent Political Thought*, New York, 1934, p. 291.

Among the textbook writers Carr, Morrison, Bernstein, and Snyder, *American Democracy in Theory and Practice*, New York, 1951, p. 24, say, "As a political system it is the mechanism through which the people govern themselves." Examples could be multiplied indefinitely. The trouble with these definitions is that they leave us deep in a bottomless pit.

Index